Dusting

for God's Fingerprints

GEORGE W. BAUM

outskirtspress
DENVER, COLORADO

Outskirts Press, Inc.
http://www.outskirtspress.com

Paperback ISBN: 978-1-4787-6430-4
Hardback ISBN: 978-1-4787-6466-3

Outskirts Press and the "OP" logo are trademarks belonging to Outskirts Press, Inc.

PRINTED IN THE UNITED STATES OF AMERICA

The story of Esther is the only book in the Bible where God's name does not appear. However, if we look at the story in retrospect, His fingerprints are all over it. And so it is, sometimes, in our lives...

Contents

For Tim Atkins
1952 – 2015
(Who had God's fingerprints all over him)

Mr. Toad's Wild Ride
Prelude

"What carts I shall fling carelessly into the ditch
in the wake of my magnificent onset!"
"O stop being an ass, Toad," cried the Mole despairingly.[1]

My personal faith journey has not been so faithful. Most of it has been "O me of little faith," and the journey has looked more like Mr. Toad's Wild Ride than anything else. I don't know how to talk about it much without Steinbeckian characters from *Cannery Row*, or somewhere *East of Eden* eating my *Grapes of Wrath*, or Murakami madness somewhere in a jazz bar in Tokyo, or Dylanesque images of the street-folk and apocalyptic apocalypse. In other words, it seems I can only talk in Dickinson truth-slant.

I was taken to Sunday School at Lincoln Park Reformed Church when I was four. I thought it was reform school, only on Sundays, so I figured I must have needed some reforming. But all I got was a vision, there in the church basement looking outside through a window to my left— some kind of call to be used of God to set something in life right. I was able to visit that space a few years ago. Couldn't see anything this time. I guess ya gotta become like a little child to see such things.

I was sick a lot in those days, which gave me time to draw pictures and become a Hardy boy trying to solve mysteries, which is what I'm still trying to do. I watched TV a lot. *The Little Rascals* provided my first understanding of ecclesiology, diverse communities, sin, and adventure. In Mayberry, Opie and Andy helped form some moral sense, and through Barney Fife, I learned to keep my bullet in my shirt pocket.

I learned that you have to behave in Sunday School. You could not roll up your clip-on tie and let it fly at the girls, and there was to be no laughing—which helped me to understand why the Pharisees never had any fun, and maybe why Jesus liked to party with sinners.

Later on, my mom dropped me off at Mt. View Gospel church, where I asked Jesus into my heart, right after pizza and basketball, and I think he came. I remember only one thing from Sunday School, from my teacher Jack Osborne: "Seek ye first the kingdom of God and his righteousness and all these things shall be added unto thee."[2] I have spent over forty years trying to figure out what that means and how to live it.

Adolescence: Holy crap! Who the heck was that creature? I played drums in a group called the Hands of Time. We entered the junior high Battle of the Bands—and we won! Our great honor was to play at the dance that night. Another group, who lost, decided to sabotage our instruments. When we came out to play, we looked like fools and could not recoup our dignity. Utterly humiliated, I spent the night against the wall with the other boys while the girls danced to records. And then a girl named Megan, cute as a button, walked all the way across the room and in front of everyone asked me to dance. It was the kindest thing that ever happened to me, and I started to believe in grace and redemption.

My dad's machine business went bust in a recession, but we were given some more grace to move to California. First, we spent the summer in Rosemead, where I was invited by some hippie chicks, Cheri and Monica, to go to the waterfalls in Azusa Canyon, drop some LSD, and get naked. I said no, and though sometimes I think I was stupid, I also think it helped somehow in my faith journey.

And then my uncle in Carlsbad invited me to stay with him for the summer.

There I believe a bridge was built to God as my Father. My uncle and aunt demonstrated care and affection in a way that paved the way to understanding God as such.

I returned home to New Jersey, was warmly welcomed by friends and girlfriend, and once more was propositioned so easily. Again I said no and again, somehow, I think it helped this faith thing. While there, I read magazines about the Jesus Movement in California. Black-and-white photographs depicted hippies, drug addicts, and a rock culture being baptized by a baldheaded preacher at Corona del Mar. I was interested, and maybe destined.

We wound up moving to California, and within three weeks I met some Jesus Freaks who took me to one of the first Maranatha concerts, in Long Beach. There I heard the simple gospel of Jesus—from that same baldheaded preacher in *Life* magazine! And I decided to follow Jesus. I had no idea that this event was to be part of the epicenter of the Jesus Movement that revolutionized modern Christianity. Long-haired, Bible-totin', and cross-bearing—I became a Jesus Freak. Guess I still am in some ways.

Premillennial, pre-tribulational rapture and apocalyptic energy surged through that movement—the "late great planet Earth." I propagated the rap to my cousin, scared her to death, and began to doubt the wisdom of this approach. Predictions of Israeli wars and end of times further caused some more thoughtful reflection on these eschatological predictions. Maybe Toad should check these things out more carefully.

I began to prepare for ministry within a church-in-the-park and at a Bible college. During my senior year I was invited to preach in a little church in an oil-field town. They hired me. I became a minister in Taft, California, at twenty-three years of age. Long-haired kid-preacher in a redneck oil patch. What a Toad!

The congregation grew, in fact tripled in three years, which I guess was something if you're Rev. Toad. But I was disillusioned with traditional church forms and began a quest within the radical sectors of Christianity, looking for authenticity. We experimented with communal living, radical politics and economics, pacifism, and Christian anarchy. I became involved in the development of a network of house churches from Seattle to San Diego. I traveled to Nicaragua during the Sandinista revolution and studied liberation theology in Mexico City at the International University with Marxist radical exiles. We interviewed the future president of Nicaragua, and saw firsthand the horrors of war and propaganda.

We started a church in the back of a bar called the Oasis, which I thought was a pretty good name for a church, and I led a bunch of middle-class folks into a mini-ghetto, attempting incarnational ministry. I saw sin and sorrow, betrayal and deceit, rape and murder, filth and filthy lucre, perversions and twisting of souls—all there on Dylan's Desolation Row.

On the House

I had fumbled my way into a very important corner of the universe—
a place where few were called, but many were funny.

It looked like a cave
but it was just a redneck bar
over on Plato Ave.

The oil patch philosophers were
holding forth in sweet converse—
calling each other "Professor" and such
with Aristotelian squeals of
Socratic dialog and verse!

There was a woman there
trying to hold up both sides
of a conversation—
who had successfully bitched
three husbands into
relative oblivion.

And that's when the brouhaha
began, over which wine
the fine young lady enjoyed most—
to which the obvious answer
was mostly other people's.

There were two brothers bellied up
to the bar, barely covering big butts without par.
And a couple of wise-ass cowboys
were flinging peanut shells toward
cracks the size of St Andreas.

It was nobody's fault
one hit the mark
and just as the brothers
rose up to defend each other's honor
I strolled in and ordered up
"Cappuccinos for everyone!"[3]

My radical phase led me to my own backyard, where several kinds of painful betrayals had occurred. Needless to say, my own life was in a revolution that I lost: wife, ministry, job, church, friends, and just about everything a person would hold dear. Empty pockets, they've got no friends (except Job—he had three of them), and Abraham—he had one: God. Well, I fell down a well, but found God at the bottom. Light shone over my left shoulder, and grace eased me on down to the bottom, and then on up. It all happened there in Toad's ditch beside the road.

I wound up back in LA, was invited to work with adult literacy and ESL programs, and began the Middle Adult chapter of my life. Within this context, I believe God wove a cocoon of healing for me. He used a group of Asian students, one of whom I wound up marrying. It took seven years, but I was eventually healed, and a butterfly emerged (or a least a toad).

I had to learn, like Joseph, to forgive those who did evil toward me, and that God, like a jazz musician, could create something good out of it all. And He did. Charlie Parker and God—blowin' riffs of redemptive analogies, right there in my soul.

I was meaning to listen to a Dodger game on the way to work, but I stumbled onto a Jewish radio host who also taught Torah at the University of Judaism; he began to help me rebuild my moral infrastructure. From there I began to read Japanese Christian authors, partly to communicate my feeble faith to my Japanese wife, and partly to view my faith from another cultural perspective. Koyama, Endo, and Kagawa helped me appreciate the faith with a new slant. So far, the journey looked like kosher sushi.

Then some folks in an area church—a minister, an associate, and a lawyer (of all things)—befriended and believed in me when I didn't have an ounce left in myself, and they helped me back into life and ministry. Some further experience in Japanese, Chinese, and Korean churches provided a few more stepping-stones toward my original calling, along with its giftings, which I am told are irrevocable.

Many streams began to flow into a river; many sticks were laid upon a fire. I experienced a profound renewal of spirit that led me back to my spiritual roots. I had to go see what I had left behind, what I had missed, so I returned to my roots—and to my first love. I saw thirty years of spiritual fruit—God's fingerprints—and sat in a coffee shop in Costa Mesa and wept.

Words to Peter were also addressed to me: "When you return, strengthen your brethren."[4]

God began to do a new, old, and deep work within me like I'd never quite experienced before. It was intimate, a divine romance; it was a fullness of God's presence that was transcendent and immanent. I was content to the bottom of my being, well within my soul. Scriptures became conversations, relationships were made new, work became creative, and family and difficult people were transformed.

This led me back into ministry again. Teaching at a Bible college, then directing the college, pastoring within a mega-church—and it was good, and there was fruit. And then I was promoted into administration, and it was bad and I saw things that made me very sad.

I was invited to an event in Oxford as an educational consultant. There, in a hotel room, I saw clearly that authoritarianism can be very toxic. I cried out with David's psalms for God to bring down justice and righteousness. But He didn't and hasn't—at least not the way and when I thought it would and should be. I became disappointed in God. I might have to wait, and with mercy. I might have to let God be God, and me be me—just a little toad after all. I think this is an important part of the faith journey.

I quit my ministry to everyone's consternation, and took a sabbatical for three months to sort it all out: life, God, vocation, work, relationships, ministry, and all things related—desperately dusting for fingerprints.

And in the process I found the Lord, my shepherd, was restoring my soul.

There was a mini-revolution at the toxic faith place. A few brave souls told Pharaoh to go to hell and were promptly fired. Sheep, good hearts, were scattered. One day out on my patio I felt the Shepherd's call to gather the scattered. So, I did. And now I had a bunch of revolutionary firecrackers meeting twice a week in my home, looking for direction and some wisdom on the faith journey.

I had to find a job again, so I went back to adult education. Déjà vu. This was where I wound up after my last ministry fiasco seventeen years earlier. They welcomed me and made a place for me. It was not the place I wanted to be, but it was a place for a misplaced toad to land.

And I also felt like I could come back to a previous church for a while. So I did, and there I have been, for the past seven years.

During this time my dad had a stroke, suffered dementia, went blind, and recently died. My wife has stage 4 breast cancer. I have a paralyzed vocal cord and Parkinson's. My best friend of thirty-five years died. And I lost my job.

My wife said, "We've both turned sixty, I have cancer, you have Parkinson's and no voice. Who the heck would want us?" My only reply: "Maybe God?" And so we've set out on an Abrahamic journey[5]— old and not knowing where we're going, but trusting that God does.

I'm tempted sometimes to give up, to give in. There's enough good reason. It all seems so sad sometimes, Mr. Toad's Wild Ride is getting weary, and yet, there are those fingerprints… Maybe there's still some good news in that old Gospel for me and you. Maybe we'll all live happily ever after, after all.

"No, no, we'll see it out," whispered Rat to Mole. "…I ought to stick by Toad till this trip is ended. It wouldn't be safe for him to be left to himself. It won't take very long. His fads never do. Good night!"[6]

Adam & Eve
Up a Tree in PV
~1~

Dear Abby,

I live in a garden paradise here in Palos Verdes—an upscale community on a peninsula south of Los Angeles—in a gated community. Part of my work is to take care of the garden. There are so many interesting plants and flowers and trees—one in particular intrigues me, but I've been told to stay away from it. And there are many kinds of animals and birds, especially peacocks. And there's the beautiful sea and so many kinds of fish. I am part zoologist, part botanist, and part marine biologist. Currently I am naming animals and birds (my favorite is the duckbilled platypus), and I'm putting them on a database in my Apple computer—and I'm inventing language as I go. It's both fascinating and fun. (I've hooked up some Bose speakers in the tree and sing along with Jimmy Buffet. My favorite song? "Cheeseburger in Paradise"—but it makes the cows a little nervous.) Life is good here in PV. But at the end of the day, something is missing. I'm a bit lonely. The animals are nice, but still I sure wish there was someone to talk to, and someone to help with all this work. Do you have any advice?

Signed, Adam of Palos Verdes

With that, Adam said his prayers and went to sleep. He had strange dreams that night. He felt like something was poking him in the ribs—must have been another unicorn dream. Named it this morning. When he woke up, the sky was blue and the sun was warm and bright. When he checked his email, he found this reply:

Dear Adam,

It sounds like you live in a wonderful place and that you have plenty of good work to do. As far as your loneliness and need for partnership, I'd go to the source. It is God who made you, like a potter out of clay. He breathed life into you that has animated your life. He's given you intelligence and creativity, freedom and responsibility—you are made in His image after all—I'd think He'd be willing to help you. In the meantime, you should probably stay away from that tree.

All the best, Abby

After Adam read his email, he got up for his morning scratch and to look for some breakfast—which was usually not too far away. But while he was reaching for a coconut, he sensed that he wasn't alone. When he turned around, there it was, moving toward him. It was like one of the animals, but not—like him in many ways, but different. What is it? he thought. What does it do? What shall I name it? "I'm a she, not an it. I, too, am made in God's image," *said She.*

Dear Abby,

I did what you said, you know, talked to God last night about my little problem. This morning I woke up with a pain in my side—and there standing in front of me was another creature looking at me with clear, beautiful eyes, with hair like mine, but long and golden. (And there were some other noticeable differences.) And then she spoke, and it was like music. I realized, *Here at last is bone of my bones, flesh of my flesh,* and I said, "Whoa, man"—and that's what I decided to call her, "Wo-man." She liked it, and responded when I talked to her. Somehow I know she's a part of me. I just wanted to thank you for your advice—and invite you to the wedding. We'll be getting married in the morning. Her Maker will be walking her down the aisle and will give her hand to me in marriage—"Holy Matrimony." She made up those words, and they sound good.

Signed, The one and only eligible bachelor in Paradise

Dear Mr. and Mrs. Adam,

Congratulations on your beautiful wedding at the Glass Chapel—and the reception at Trump Resort was wonderful. Now the two of you will become one. "For this reason a man shall leave his father and mother and cleave to his wife."[7] Enjoy your honeymoon.

Signed, Abby

Now the serpent was more subtle than any other wild creature that the Lord God had made.

Dear Abby,

We had a wonderful honeymoon. I now have a helper, a partner, and I'm no longer lonely. Life is good. Having this oneness in a relationship makes the garden more beautiful, the food tastes better shared, and work is more meaningful together. But soon after we got home, my wife began talking to a serpent near the tree—or rather listening, I should say. She comes home after work and tells me what they talked about, and I am getting concerned.

Bub, what we call him, questions what God has told us about the tree. I think he shrewdly disguises a challenge in what seems like an innocent question. "Has God said?" he queries. It makes us think about God's prohibitions. My wife told the serpent we shouldn't eat of the tree in the middle of the garden, neither touch it, or we'd die. Then the serpent raised up on his back legs and hissed, "You will not die! God knows that when you eat of the tree, your eyes will be opened, you will be like God, knowing and deciding what is good and what is evil."[8] Might this be true?

My wife has been taking walks down by that tree each day, and now I've been going with her. Every day it looks more enticing, and our mouths begin to water when we see it. It seems like a magnet pulling us. Maybe we *can* be like God. We're not getting much work done these days. Seems like all we can think and talk about these days is that tree. What do you think we should do, Abby?

Signed, Up a Tree in PV

Dear Adam,

My advice: stay away from that tree. God gave you everything else in the garden. It's all a gift to you both. You've only been prohibited *one* thing—I know that might make you want it even more, but don't listen to that snake, Bub—it's all a lie. But the choice and the consequences are yours.

Signed, Abby

The next day, when the woman was window-shopping near the tree, she saw that it was a delight to her eyes—and it would be good to eat—and when she thought she could become wise, like God, she took of its fruit and ate. And she also gave some to her husband.

Dear Abby,

Something has gone terribly wrong! Everything looks different, and we feel really strange—like we need to hide from each other. We have had to invent new words for these feelings. I call it guilt; she calls it shame. We don't talk much anymore—at least, not without an argument.

We've started a new sewing business making clothes to cover us. They're made of fig leaves. The problem is they itch. In fact, everything is irritating these days. It feels like something has been lost, something has fallen, something has broken. It feels like life has come apart at the seams. It doesn't feel good. Nothing seems right. Everything's gone wrong. I've even been listening to country music lately.

This evening, in the cool of the day, we heard the sound of footsteps coming. We were afraid. We thought it might be Bub or the Boogie Man. They were large footsteps. They were God's footsteps. We ran. We hid. And it wasn't a game. What can we do now, Abby?

Signed, Lost in Paradise

That day Adam got another email with a YouTube link: There was no image, just a voice crying out, "Where are you?" And it was signed—"God."

Dear God,

I heard the sound of you in the garden and I was afraid, because I was naked, and I hid myself.

Shamefully, Adam

Dear Adam,

Who told you that you were naked? Have you eaten of the tree which I commanded you not to eat?

Dear God,

The woman—whom *you* gave to be with me—*she* gave me fruit from the tree—and I ate it.

Dear Mrs. Adam,

What is this you have done?

Dear God,

The serpent beguiled me, and I ate.

We then saw Bub slithering by, with no more feet, eating dust and hissing something vile at my wife about crushing her future seed.

Dear Abby,

Things sure are different these days because we chose to listen to lies, the lust of our eyes and flesh, and we let our pride take over. We wanted to be like God, to know it all, to call our own shots. Pretty foolish for a couple of people made of mud.

My wife is pretty grouchy these days. She keeps finding ways to try to control me, but I tell her, "I'm the man and what I say goes"—which doesn't go over very well. I think we need some counseling—but the first one we listened to led us astray.

As for me, work stinks—part of my consequences, I'm told. I have to work longer days, sweat more, and I get less return on my investment—maybe I need to join a union.

Most nights when I get home, she starts nagging. So I've started going to the Bull Pen (a local bar) before I get home—hoping it will numb my sense of Paradise lost.

Something new has happened in our home. My wife made a new creature—it was very painful, and she blamed me, but out of her came a little person. He looks a little like her and a little like me—he is made in our image. He cries a lot and eats a lot, but something is new and there's something new between us, besides changing diapers. I now call her Eve, "the one who gives life."

We are now living outside the gated community, actually in Lomita. All the roads to PV have been blocked. God says he didn't want us to live forever in this fallen condition. With all the mess we've caused, God still cares for us and shows us mercy. He even got some new clothes for us from the House of Suede—sure better than those pathetic fig leaves we made ourselves.

So I guess we'll settle down here, work the hard land, work on our relationships—with God and with each other, and here we'll raise a little Cain.

Yours truly, Adam

And the rest, as they say, is history…

Dear Abby,

I feel a lot like Adam much of the time. Is there any hope for someone like me?

Signed, Jack—often up a tree—in more than PV

Dear Jack,

This is not the end of your story. *Look for His fingerprints!*

Signed, Abby

Remembering How to Laugh
~2~

Old Abe was well-to-do, his stock portfolio well diversified, bets all hedged, and it would seem he had found the elusive comfort zone. Seems he'd bought some fine horse property up in Rolling Hills Estates. Had a big screen, hi-def TV all cabled up to watch a bunch of grown men freeze their hind ends off chasing around a pigskin for a whole pile of money.

Now, where seldom was heard a discouraging word, one came to Abe— right at half-time. The phone rang and Sara said, "Abe, it's for you." And God, who'd left his fingerprints all over Abe's life, had something to say. "Get up and go—to a place you don't know." (Imagine: God interrupting right in the middle of a playoff game.) "I'm going to bless you and you're going to be a blessing to a whole bunch of folks you'll never know."[9] Abe was listening, but also mumbling something about God's sense of humor. But he packed up and headed to who-knows-where—the same place where some of our lives wind up on this faith journey.

Everyone thought he was nuts, especially Sara, but she was battling menopause, which can make anyone a little nutty. And in between hot flashes, God made a birth announcement (seemed like he was biting his tongue to keep from laughing): It would seem that soon Ol' Sara would be doing a split-shift between the retirement home and maternity ward. And all that was left to do now was remember how to laugh: For while Abraham and Sara waited for their pension checks and Medicare to come through, they were also waiting for the stork to arrive, and for the fulfillment of God's promise—one that would impact all of history.

So, Ol' Abe and Ol' Sara left home for a new land, painted the nursery, and stocked up on Geritol and Pampers, fiber and formula, pacifiers and prunes. In the face of all this craziness, Sara laughed—silently to herself: *How can a worn-out old woman like me enjoy such pleasure, especially when my husband is also so old?* (Viagra had not yet been invented.) And God called her on it, saying: "Why did Sara laugh? Why did she say, 'Can an old woman like me have a baby?' Is anything too hard for the Lord?" And then God said, "About this time next year, I will return, and Sara will have a son."

Sara was afraid, and denied it, saying, "I didn't laugh." But the Lord said, "No, but you did laugh." It was the laughter of unbelief.

And, one year later, God did just what he promised—for a son was born. And Sara declared, "God has brought *me* laughter. All who hear about this will laugh with me." And the baby was named Isaac, which means, of course, laughter. This time her laughter was born of faith.

It's important to remember how to laugh. Sometimes life gets overwhelming, we take ourselves too seriously—we forget to laugh. I found myself in this situation a few weeks ago. As I walked through the parking lot, I realized I hadn't laughed for a long time. In my car I put on a comedy station. I began to smile, then chuckle, giggle, and soon full-blown laughter and tears. Boy, it felt good. I thought back over my life—and all the times I'd forgotten to laugh.

It's important to laugh. Even the existentially despairing book of Ecclesiastes says, "There is a time to cry and a time to laugh." (Sometimes we're not sure which.) Wise Solomon knew: Laughter is the best medicine. Norman Cousins at UCLA discovered that endorphins are a natural painkiller. Laughter produces endorphins. Hence, laughter therapy for cancer patients was born. Laughter can be a spiritual weapon, break the tension, help us get perspective on things. And God enjoys our laughter. As parents we enjoy our children's smiles and laughter—how much more must God enjoy ours!

It is important to laugh—and important to laugh for the right reasons. From our Sara story, it would seem that there are two kinds of laughter: laughter that proceeds from faith, and laughter that comes from unfaith. Sara laughed, at first, because she did not believe God would or could do what was promised. Later she laughed in belief and wonder at God's faithfulness. George MacDonald has said it well: *"It's the heart that is not yet sure of its God that is afraid to laugh in His presence."*

Laughter from unfaith can be empty or foolish (just listen to laugh tracks added to sitcoms). It is because we don't know where to find real joy. One product of a relationship with God is joy—and its cousin, laughter! Laughter from unfaith can take many forms: cynical laughter (a loss of hope due to loss of faith), mockery, scorn, laughing *at* someone. When Jesus said a little girl was not dead, just sleeping, people laughed at him in unbelief. Laughter can be a way to exclude, reject, or lower someone on a pecking order.

Laughter that comes from faith is the kind that laughs with God, like Sara. It begins with humility, the mother of many virtues. It is an accurate estimate of myself before God and people. In humility I'm able to laugh at myself—not take myself too seriously.

"Angels can fly because they can take themselves lightly. Pride is the downward drag into any easy solemnity. One settles down into a selfish seriousness—but a person needs to rise to self-forgetfulness. Seriousness is not a virtue. It's really a natural trend into taking one's self gravely—because it's the easiest thing to do. Seriousness flows out of people naturally; but laughter is a leap of faith. It's easy to be heavy; hard to be light. Satan fell by the force of gravity."[10]

Friends and family usually are willing to help us laugh at ourselves. My kids will never let me forget the time I set myself on fire reaching for lasagna or when I temporarily went blind from wiping a jalapeño pepper in my eye. And there was the time when I was a teacher and my desk chair tipped over and landed on my head. Those who saw will never let me forget—helping me to laugh at myself.

Laughter born of faith is confident that God is at work in our lives. (We've seen His fingerprints.) Faith delights that things work together for good for those who love God. Joy does not escape sorrow—but sorrow cannot drive out the joy of those whose confidence is in God. Though we all have, and will have, tears, laughter for a believer will ultimately trump those tears. And so, with Sara, we can laugh with confidence in God at work.

Faith gives birth to courage, which gives us strength to laugh in the midst of whatever we go through. Into the valley of the shadow of death we all travel. The courage of faith hears a whisper: "Knock, Knock." "Who's there?" And faith finds there really is Someone there—God, with us and for us. It's evidence of things hoped for, conviction of things not seen.

Courage heads to the chemo ward and throws a picnic, and there she laughs in the face of fear—and it's often contagious—encouraging others. Courage rides on the cancer shuttle bus and along the way makes hats, makes friends, makes jokes—speaks faith language in the face of impossibilities.

The laughter of faith is a glimpse of heaven, an anticipation of future joy. "Those who sow in tears will reap with songs of joy."[11] And Jesus promised, "Blessed are you who weep now, for you shall laugh."[12]

"That means not just that you shall laugh when the time comes but that you can laugh a little even now in the midst of the weeping because you know that the time is coming"[13] "Christians are people who know that complexity and struggle are the name of the game, but who party like 5 year-olds when hope arrives."[14] Yes, "Joy is the serious business of heaven."[15]- And Joy's cousin, laughter, is a glimpse of heaven.

The world can get a bit overwhelming at times, and we can take ourselves too seriously. So, it's important to remember to laugh. The Good News is we *can* laugh - because God in Christ has the last laugh—and he who laughs last - laughs best!

Joey's Equation
~3~

Joey came down late for breakfast, having been engrossed in a night of wonderfully vivid dreams. His eleven brothers were finishing up their breakfast and morning newspaper when the younger Joey made his entrance. Papa Jake said to his wife, "Rachel, fix a nice bagel with lox and extra cream cheese for our son, the doctor." Now Joey was no doctor; he was just out of high school, though he was very interested in psychoanalysis, especially dream interpretation—and also equations.

His brothers uttered a few nasty sibling remarks about the "favorite son." It didn't help that Joey was wearing the fancy coat his dad had given him—and only him. It was of the finest weave, monogrammed with princely sleeves. The brothers cursed a while and then headed out for work in the sheep pasture.

Now after breakfast, and an extra cup of venti non-fat latte with a couple of shots for his favorite son, Jake sent Joey out to check on his brothers—which went over a little like a pork chop at a bar mitzvah. Joey, like many younger brothers, enjoyed this tattletale progress report to Dad, but not half as much as what he had up his precious sleeve *this* morning.

"Hey, you guys!" Little Joe called to his brothers.

"Oh, God—here he comes again. Let's ditch him!" they said, but Joey was too quick; and he could hardly contain himself.

"You'll never guess what!"

"What?" said a couple of them in disgust.

"Last night I had a dream and you were all in it! There we all were, tying up bundles of wheat in the field. And guess what! My bundle rose up and stood upright. Then your bundles gathered around it and... and...and bowed down to my bundle. Isn't that cool!"

"That's a bundle, all right," said Simeon. "A load of—" Another brother said, "Are *you* going to rule over *us*? When hell freezes over!" (In reality the heat was being turned up.) The brothers hated him even more because of his dreams.

But Joey, so absorbed in his dreams and himself, and not realizing he was about two steps from being thrown in a ditch, had a second dream to tell them about. Now, in the ancient world, dreams were thought to be messages from God and if you had a second similar dream, they gained credibility. So, Joey fired away:

"Look, there was the sun, okay, and the moon, right, and eleven stars were bowing down *to me*!"

"That's it!" said all the other brothers. "We've had it!" And when Joey the Oblivious told the dream to his father, even his dad scolded him. "What kind of dream is that? Shall we come, your mother and brothers and I, and bow down before you?" (Hebrew = "Vaddya, nuts?")

So his brothers were jealous of him. But his father kept the matter in mind. To his wife he said, "Rachel, I think the young one, the dreamer, might need a little counseling."

The next day Joey was sent out to report on his brothers again. But they were still ticked mightily. They saw him coming and hatched a plan to give him the shank and throw him in a ditch, leave him there, and let the wild animals eat him. "We'll see then what becomes of his dreams!" (And they surely would.)

But Reuben, the eldest, intervened and said, "Let's not kill him, just leave him in the ditch." (He had his own plan to rescue Joey and bring him home.)

So when Joey got there, probably working on a new dream to tell them, the brothers jumped him, ripped off that silly coat, and threw him in a pit, which was really an old well with no water in it.

Then they had lunch (so Scriptures say).

While they were eating, they saw a caravan of traders coming, on their way to Egypt. Brother Judah, the entrepreneur, said, "What profit is it if we leave our brother in a ditch to die? Let's sell him to these guys, divvy up the profit, and buy our own darn coats." And for the first time all the brothers agreed (all except the one in the ditch). So, they sold their brother out for twenty pieces of silver, made up a sad story to tell dear old Dad, and they made it all look like an accident.

And Papa Jake grieved and mourned for his favorite son and refused to be comforted.

Well, Joey wound up down in Egypt and lucked into a good job working for Mr. Potiphar, an officer of the head cheese, the Pharaoh. And God was with Joey and he became a successful man. The Lord caused everything to prosper in his hands and therefore he was put in charge, trusted to take care of everything—everything, that is, except for Mrs. Potiphar.

Now Joey was a handsome man—we are told—and Mrs. P had been watching too much *50 Shades of Grey*. She started batting her eyes at young Joe—"How you doin'?"—and day after day she made a play for him. But Joey knew better than to get caught up in this Lipstick Jungle—so he ran like hell, leaving his favorite coat with the monogram behind (which is all you could see as he ran out of the palace).

Well, as you might guess, Mrs. P, to save face, cried rape and then called her lawyer. When Mr. P got home, the Mrs. concocted quite a story with lots of drama—with a few Jewish racial slurs thrown in for effect.

As you can imagine, this all fried Mr. P's bacon and he threw Joey in the clink. But the Lord was with Joey—even there. And he received favor. He just kept landing on his feet—in fact he kind of ran the prison after a while, which gave him an opportunity to work on his equations.

While he was there, two of the king's servants (a cupbearer and a baker) who had offended the king had some wild dreams and Joseph was able to interpret them. They eventually got out of jail, but forgot about their dream analyst.

But one day, when the Pharaoh had a pretty complex dream (which none of his $500-an-hour shrinks could figure out), they remembered Joseph. Joey had Pharaoh lie on the couch and cracked the symbol code of the dream—which was that there were going to be seven years of prosperity, followed by seven years of famine. He calculated a plan to save Egypt. He was good at equations.

And this is how Joey's brothers wound up going down to Egypt. And to get some grain, they had to go through—guess who? That old dreamer who had become Pharaoh's right-hand man. And Joey's brothers came and bowed before him, but they did not know it was him.

Joey then remembered his dreams, but something in him had changed. He knew the old equation that went something like: "You threw me under the bus, so time plus opportunity equals 'I will make you pay.' It's only fair to balance the equation." The problem was, things kept escalating, and there never was a balance to the equation. But Joey came up with a new, more powerful equation:

"God has sent me ahead of you to keep you and your families alive and to preserve many survivors." But Joseph replied, "Don't be afraid of me. Am I God, that I can punish you? You intended to harm me, but God intended it all for good. He brought me to this position so I could save the lives of many people. No, don't be afraid. I will continue to take care of you and your children." So he reassured them by speaking kindly to them."

Genesis 45:7 + 50:19-21 (NLT)

Somehow Joey had figured out that the missing variable of the old equation was God. When Joey recognized God's fingerprints as He worked behind the scenes in his life, everything changed. He saw his brothers with new eyes. His perspective on the pit, the prison, and Mrs. Potiphar was transformed. He saw that God was up to something. In Joey's new equation, God was creatively working all the bad things in his life into something good—into something bigger and better and for everyone's benefit. This was Joey's equation.

Learning Joey's Equation

- New equations are worked out in the **pit**—the pit of betrayal, helplessness, fear, and abandonment. There in the pit, we begin to reach out for help. When hitting bottom, we tend to look up—and something can begin to change. We begin to work on new equations.
- New equations are figured out in **pain**—the pain of being sold out by those you thought should love and care for you, the

pain of illness and irrationality, and of loss and the many sufferings we face. We have choices to make and opportunities to trace God's fingerprints and add them to our equation.

- New equations are developed in **temptations and testings.** They provide opportunities to strengthen. They let us know whether the bridge of our character is strong enough to drive over. They help us test whether our new equations are plausible.

- New equations are developed in **prisons** (great literature and a large part of the New Testament were written from prisons). Prisons are places where we do not want to be—places where we get stuck—and it all seems so unfair. In our prisons we are sometimes given opportunities to think and to pray and to work out different equations, which might include other people's dreams.

- New equations are lived out in **prosperity.** Joey remembers the dreams given, but approaches them now with some humility carved out of the pain, the pit, and the prison. Gratitude is part of the equation. And with prosperity comes a responsibility for others who are working out their equations.

And then God enters the equation: God comes in humility, choosing to be vulnerable and transparent, grieving over our sin—that which separates us. For God seeks relationship more than anything else. God is not blind to sin—he looks us straight in the face, sees the hurt we've experienced and the harm we have caused, and calls it what it is. But there's something in his eyes, something different. God seeks our ultimate well-being, and He has a bigger picture in view. Therefore, He goes to work on His own equations to save us from our sins and from ourselves and from each other—what has been planned for evil, He "plans it over for good" (Hebrew). God is always working on a new equation.

Jesus recognizes the fingerprints and takes the Joseph story all the way to the cross: "Father, forgive them; they know not what they have done." What Jesus' brothers meant for evil, God meant for good—our salvation. Resurrection is the final word to any form of death. It is a new equation from which to live.

Later, **Paul** would connect the dots between Joseph and Jesus and his own life and say, "God is working in all things for the good..." That's our work today—to connect the dots—to work out the equations in our life challenges.

The Good News is that God can be the determining value in our equations. And this makes all the difference.

"God is too good to be unkind. He is too wise to be confused.
If I cannot trace his hand, I can always trust his heart."[16]

So, it doesn't matter if others have caused our loss and sufferings—or whether we've brought them on ourselves. There's a more important variable in the equation of our lives. That variable is God. Check the fingerprints. This is Joey's equation. *Go figure!*

Redemptive Winks

~4~

The Lord gave another message to Jeremiah.
He said, "Go down to the potter's shop, and I will speak to you there."
So I did as he told me and found the potter working at his wheel.
But the jar he was making did not turn out as he had hoped,
so he crushed it into a lump of clay again and started over.
Then the Lord gave me this message:
"O Israel, can I not do to you as this potter has done to his clay?
As the clay is in the potter's hand, so are you in my hand."[17]

Sometimes we wonder if we are alone in all of this, if God is in this thing with us or not. And then comes along some kind of wink from God, some fingerprint, and that changes everything...

Jeremiah

His name was Jeremiah, and he *was* a kind of bullfrog—but that came later on a Three-Dog Night. Originally he was a priest's kid until God roped him into being his bullfrog, croaking out the Word of Yahweh, God of Israel, trying to rope the Israelites back into being faithful to their God. Later on he went into real estate. (Read the book—it's all there.) Israel, God's people, had been in a mighty mess of sin.

But one day, in the middle of a nap, a word came from the Lord to Jeremiah. Now, he had learned to keep his antenna up for such things, even while doing ordinary things.

"Get up and go down to the potter's house, and there I will let you hear my words." Jeremiah had learned that it is only in obeying these

kinds of words that one can hear clearly God's word, and so the bull-frog hopped on down to the potter's house.

There the potter was working at his wheel, getting his lump of clay centered, pumping the wheel to spin, positioning his hands upon the creation he had in mind. Just another ordinary day in the potter's house.

Jeremiah had learned not just to listen, but to observe carefully in or-der to understand the Word of the Lord. And this is what he observed: the vessel that the potter was making was spoiled in the potter's hand—it was all messed up, marred. But the story was not over. God was about to wink.

Jeremiah continued to watch and listen for the Word of God in this or-dinary event, and he saw the potter's skillful hands now reworking the marred pot into another vessel—as it seemed good to the potter to do.

And then the Word of the Lord came to Jeremiah: *"Oh people of God, can I not do with you as the potter has done?"* declared the Lord. *"Behold, like the potter's hand, so are you in my hand, O people of God."*[18]

And Jeremiah, the bullfrog, went forth, croaking this Word to any who would listen: those with antennae up, those willing to listen and obey, those who would observe God's fingerprints on the ordinary, doing the extraordinary, even with those who were marred—making something good out of the bad. This is a story of redemption, and sometimes redemption winks.

Paul

Many years later there was a man named Paul, whom they used to call Saul. He had a lot on the ball, brilliant, multilingual, multicul-tural, and all.

He reminds me a little of Al Pacino: short, intense, and clever. But Paul mistook serving God for being a godfather, just like Al, and he had some of God's people fitted for cement shoes and thrown in the River Jordan—and not to be baptized.

Pauly thought he was doing what was best for God by arresting Christians. (A lot of harm is done in the name of doing good.) He was feared above all of the Jerusalem mafia families known as the Pharisees.

But the Potter had other plans for this marred vessel.

On the way to Damascus, Saul was knocked for a loop by a great light, which blinded him. There his antenna shot up, and he humbly began to listen to the Word of God more clearly. Through a series of events, the Potter began to refashion the marred Saul into the new Paul. And through Jesus glasses he came to learn God was not a godfather, but rather God our father, and Paul began to behave accordingly.

Paul went away for a while into a witness protection plan out in the desert, hosted by a family of those he'd murdered—the Christians. Imagine Don Corleone coming to live in your house. (I'd keep an eye on the horses.)

There Paul learned to listen to God more carefully, to obey more humbly, and to observe that the marred clay upon the wheel was himself, and that, behold, God was making a new vessel—one that would introduce the good news of redemption to the whole western world.

Here is how he would say it: *"God works all things into good—for those who love him and are called according to his purpose."*[19]

Those are redemptive words, and mighty good words for those of us whose lives have been messed up in one way or another.

Jeremiah and Paul bear witness to the same redemptive God. Others in our history will add their stories—all of them telling of a God who works all things into good. And some will even say that God sometimes winks.

Definitions

- **Redemption** = to buy back from captivity, slavery, to ransom, to repair and restore. Savings bonds, Green Stamps, slaves, clay pots, and people who are messed up can all be redeemed.
- **Winking** = a gesture that indicates somehow we understand each other, even if everyone else is oblivious.
- **Redemptive winks** = when God does something in your life and somehow you and God understand what's going on, even if no one else does.

A redemptive wink can be some kind of event that seems to be more than coincidence, or a particular kind of encouragement that is meaningful to us, or some kind of signpost of assurance that God is with us, for us, and is helping us on our journey—redeeming our lives like the marred pot, or the murderer Saul—God, making something new, making someone new, weaving all things together for good with redeeming grace—and leaving fingerprints!

Some Redemptive Winks

Emmett Kelly, Jr.

Growing up near NYC, I had the wonderful privilege to go to Madison Square Garden to see Barnum & Bailey's circus. My favorite part was the clowns, especially one named Emmett Kelly. He was famous for sweeping the spotlight into a dustpan, and his registered sad-clown face told parables.

Upon learning of her father's death, Stasia Kelley boarded a plane for Sarasota. The night before she had talked to her dad. He had been somewhat out of character, reminiscing about his life. He said the day he asked her mother to marry him and the day Stasia was born were the happiest days of his life. Emmett guarded his trademark frown so carefully that the only picture of him smiling was by a photographer on the day of Stasia's birth.

As Stasia was sitting on the plane, she had a copy of the morning paper and an old paper with the picture of her dad smiling. She reflected on the picture and it struck her that he was smiling about her—and she began to cry. The man on the plane next to her asked if she was all right. She whispered "yes" and that her father had died that morning. The man's face turned ashen as he told Stasia he was the one who took the picture. And a peace suddenly overcame her and she felt that her father was by God's side, smiling at her. The photographer, Frank Beatty, and Stasia became good friends. He was even the photographer at her wedding.[20]

I believe God winked at Stasia and that it was redemptive—and in her telling, it became a redemptive wink of God toward me.

NJ to CA

I grew up in New Jersey. Due to my dad's job, we moved to California in the middle of my high school year. Several months before, I was reading *Life* magazine, intrigued with the "Jesus Movement" in California. Hundreds of hippies and young people were being baptized at Corona del Mar—many by an older bald man.

Later we moved to California, and within three weeks I met some Jesus Freaks. They invited me to a rock concert in Long Beach. Sitting in the balcony I was impressed with the music and the Christian words. At the end a man walked out, Bible in hand. It was the same bald man from the magazine! (Wink.) He shared a simple message of God's love and invited people to follow Jesus. Hundreds accepted the invitation—I was one.

Pop

Recently, as my dad lay dying, I visited him to say goodbye. It reminded me of the time I had visited his dad on his deathbed. He was not conscious, but I decided to say a few words anyway, "Pop—I just wanted you to know God loves you. And no matter what you've done, you are forgiven because of Jesus." At that, he sat up, winked, and went back to sleep—dying shortly thereafter—a redemptive wink it would seem.

In all this, somehow God winked and I knew He was in it with us, and for us. Working to make something good out of all things—even cancer.

Do you have such stories? Are they just coincidences? Maybe. I'm sure math folks could calculate the probabilities. But there seems to be something more, and I think all of it together should be factored into the equation.

Redemptive winks do not have to be spectacular, miraculous, or even coincidental. Sometimes they are just ordinary acts of caring at the needed time: an encouraging note or call, a hand on your shoulder when you needed it, a gift of a meal and shared friendship, a thoughtful gift, an act of quiet service, a simple gesture of kindness. They can be God's winks, and they can be very redemptive.

We can learn with Jeremiah to keep our antennae up for such things, to listen, to observe carefully, and then to become a redemptive agent of God in this world like Paul, telling our stories about how *"God works all things together for good to those who love him and are called according to his purpose."*

Conclusion:

Jazz, for me, is a redemptive media. In jazz there is a theme/melody along with a chord progression (like the initial creativity of Genesis 1 and 2).

But this follows with disharmony and discord (like the fall of humanity in Genesis 3).

In the rest of the song, jazz musicians are working toward resolution of discord—redemption—bringing something good out of it all, like a marred pot on a potter's wheel, like a murderer on the road to Damascus. The musicians are working with each other and their audience to make a new pot, a new man. Jazz can be redemptive.

One more wink, and I'll be still:

It has been told of Wynton Marsalis[21] that he visited a jazz club in Greenwich Village where some young musicians were holding forth. At the break, Wynton was invited to sit in on the next set. Now, when you play with someone so much better, you tend to get better—and so it was this night. The young cats were finding their groove—pretty soon jumpin' and smokin'—on into a sweet blues solo by Mr. Marsalis—when all of a sudden someone's cell phone went off, with one of those annoying tunes. The crowd gasped. But Wynton did not miss a beat. He began to play the cell tune—and he played it nine different ways! (Now there's a redemptive wink!)

And so are we in the Potter's hand. Indeed, God works all things together for good—and He does it with a wink, for His fingerprints are all over us!

The Language of Grace
(As Overheard in a Blues Club)
~5~

The water rose over my head,
and I cried out, "This is the end!"

But I called on your name, Lord,
from deep within the pit.

You heard me when I cried, "Listen to my pleading!
Hear my cry for help!"

Yes, you came when I called;
you told me, "Do not fear."[21]

Grace is a place like a blues club in Watts where I have hung out from time to time. There you'll find an older gentleman, eighty years young, sporting a fine derby, decked to the nines and announcing, "I am the host!"—greeting each guest warmly. Grace is welcoming, and most hospitable.

There was a ninety-year-old lady named Babe who owned and opened the club just for the life of it—which is an act of grace, it would seem. And there's the house band, "Mighty Balls of Fire" they call themselves—cats a jammin', offering up the blues for all to hear. A gift to be sure.

Ya never know who might show up in these places; grace is always full of surprises. Most blues folks have been through there one time or another. Of course there's Miss Mickey beltin' out them blues—with a voice three parts Hennessey, one part acetylene torch. "God's a cryin' out for His people," says she (thereby preaching Grace whether she knows it or not, which is also some more grace). And she's a struttin' her stuff between what's left of a few broken teeth—and telling the stories, always the stories, and declaring, "I am your living legend." Sometimes she gets confused with the Christ, but it's okay, Grace doesn't mind—God's busy enjoying the music, the folks, the fried chicken, and the jokes—like the young white boy next to me who says he doesn't know why they call it the blues when it makes him happy. He's learning you don't "get into the blues," but you play the blues to get out of them. Grace, overheard in a blues club.

Just like another young man backstage, picking and sliding out some blues riffs, humming a sad tune, and singing his story. An old story, 'bout 2,600 years old—calls it Jeremiah's Blues, and it's played in every minor key.

1st Stanza: The song begins soon after 586 BC, with a lamentation of grief over a most tragic destruction of Jerusalem. These are the blues, moaning and mourning the exile of God's people into slavery in Babylon—for seventy years…

"Jerusalem, once so full of people, is now deserted.
She who once was great among the nations now sits alone
Once a queen now a slave
She sobs through the night—tears stream down her cheeks.
Among all her chosen lovers and friends there is none to comfort her
She has been led away to captivity, now oppressed with a cruel enslavement.
She has no place of rest."[23]

Seems God and His people had been in a committed relationship together. But His people went after other gods, violated the covenant relationship with Yahweh. They had turned from the ethical monotheism of the covenant and worshiped other gods, embraced contrary values, lived unfaithfully toward their God. *(Let the blues harp wail in a much lesser key.)*

God warned them through the crazy prophets many a time,
YHWH, the brokenhearted God, called for his beloved to come back in oh so many ways.
(Hush now, children, for we're on sacred ground.)

Oh, but Jerusalem resisted—said no to God a thousand times. She chose to indulge in her most favorite sins.
(You can just hear the strings bending till they almost break.)

And now after every effort to bring her back, God takes his hands off His people. He lets them go; they are free to choose their own way.

Now with that gracious hand off, other bad hands come in—and all hell breaks loose—thanks to Babylon and company.

But there, still there, watching, waiting in the shadows—peeking from behind the curtain—is our God. Ready to forgive, ready to restore, ready to bring grace, if any is desired.

2nd Stanza of Jeremiah's blues (Lam 2) speaks of captured children and the majesty of Jerusalem stripped away, the sacred Temple violated, people groaning for bread, defiled by immorality, lying in the gutter with no one to help—their enemies mock them. There is weeping and no one to comfort, no sense of future, no longer any hope. These are indeed the blues, but they are also potential places of grace—places our God often shows up.

3rd Stanza: The singer's life becomes woven into the people's (you might find yourself in this part of the song) and now he sings:

> *"I am the one who has seen afflictions*
> *I have been led into darkness, there is no light.*
> *God has turned his hand against me*
> *He has made my skin grow old*
>
> *I am surrounded with anguish and stress*
> *I feel walled in, and I cannot escape*
> *Bound in heavy chains*
> *And though I cry and shout, he has shut out my prayers*
>
> *He has blocked my way, he has made my way crooked*
> *He has shot arrows deep into my heart*
> *I am filled with bitterness for I've been given a bitter cup of sorrow*
> *to drink*
>
> *All peace is gone, I've forgotten what good times were like*
> *I cry out because my strength and my hope are gone*
> *Everything I had hoped for from the Lord is gone.*
> *The thought of my suffering is beyond words*
> *I will never forget this awful time as I grieve over my loss.*
> ***And Yet...*** *"*[24]

The blues are now in full swing. And he is singing our song, giving us words for our own laments. *"And yet..."* Oh my—just a little contrasting conjunction busting into this blues tune opens a crack in the door to hope.

"Yet, I still dare to hope..." says the prophet.

Why or how? When I **remember** this:

> *"The faithful love of the Lord never ends*
> *His mercies never cease*
> *They are new every morning*
> *Great is Thy faithfulness*
> *The Lord is my portion, my inheritance*
> *Therefore I will hope in him."*[25]

The Hebrew blues singer's lament turns on a little word, *"yet."*

The key that turns the lament is his memory of God's grace in the history of Israel, and the faithfulness of God throughout his own story. He remembers. And therefore he hopes in the steadfast love, the mercy and faithfulness of God. Memories of grace are ushered in by the word "yet" in the very midst of the blues.

He is learning the language of grace—as overheard in a blues club.

What is this Grace spoken of ? It is pure gift.

F. Buechner: "A crucial eccentricity of the Christian faith is the assertion that people are saved by grace. There is *nothing* you have to do. There's nothing you *have* to do. There's nothing you have to *do*.

"There's only one catch. Like any other gift, the gift of grace can be yours only if you'll reach out and take it."[26]

I once got front-center row tickets to a Dylan/Santana concert the day before for very cheap. (Bill Walton sat behind me and when he found out what I paid for better seats than his, he razzed me the whole time.) I had to leave after Dylan, so I tried to give the ticket to someone—free. Everyone looked at me like I was a Colombian drug dealer, so I went to the very last row, found a young man alone, and offered him the free ticket. He looked at me skeptically. Then he said,

"Really?" And he grabbed the ticket and ran. I waited and watched as he found the front-row seat. He then looked back at me, waved, and shook his head in disbelief. It's hard to give away grace.

What is this Grace spoken of? It is extravagant. It goes beyond.

Fiorello LaGuardia was the mayor of New York City during some of the worst days of the Great Depression and all of World War II. He was adoringly called "the Little Flower" by the people of New York because he stood only five foot four and always wore a carnation in his lapel.

He was a colorful character. Sometimes he would ride the New York City fire trucks. Sometimes he would go with the police when they raided the speakeasies. He would take entire orphanages to a baseball game. Once he went on the radio during a newspaper strike and read the comics to the children.

One really cold night in January of 1935, he showed up at night court in the poorest ward of the city and dismissed the judge for the evening, taking over the bench himself. A tattered old woman was brought before him. She was charged with stealing a loaf of bread. Her daughter was sick and her grandchildren were starving. But the shopkeeper, from whom she stole the bread, refused to drop the charges, stating: "It's a real bad neighborhood, Your Honor. She's got to be punished to teach other people around here a lesson."

LaGuardia sighed as if deep in thought. Finally, he turned to the woman and said, "I've got to punish you. The law makes no exceptions—ten dollars or ten days in jail."

(*God's grace justifies the sinner, but not the sin. That would be cheap grace.*)

But, even as he was pronouncing the sentence, he was reaching into his pocket. He took out a ten-dollar bill and tossed it into his famous hat, saying: "Here is the ten-dollar fine, which I now remit; and furthermore I am going to fine everyone in this courtroom fifty cents for living in a town where a person has to steal bread so that her grandchildren can eat. Mr. Bailiff, collect the fines and give them to the defendant."

The following day the newspapers reported that $47.50 was turned over to the bewildered woman who had stolen a loaf of bread to feed her starving grandchildren, fifty cents of it being contributed by the red-faced grocery store owner, while some seventy petty criminals, people with traffic violations, and New York City police officers, each paid fifty cents and then gave the mayor a standing ovation.[27]

Grace is extravagant. It goes beyond.

What is this Grace spoken of? It is something that has the power to turn your life right-side up.

"Amazing Grace! How sweet the sound that saved a wretch like me! I once was lost, but now am found; was blind, but now I see."

John Newton penned the words to this wonderful hymn. He was a minister in the Church of England at the time. But, prior to becoming a Christian minister, he was a sailor who was kicked out of the British navy because he was, to put it mildly, one bad dude. He became a sea captain of a merchant ship like his father before him. The cargo of his ship was slaves. He was a cruel shipmaster who profited from the selling of human flesh. While slave trading was a real moneymaker for him, it was a wretched and miserable life for the slaves.

Following a terrible storm that struck fear in everyone on Newton's ship, including him, he began to think about his need for God. He wrote of this turning point, "I can see no reason why God singled me out for mercy, unless it was to show, by one astonishing instance, that with God nothing is impossible."

Newton read a pamphlet from John Wesley and was convinced of the moral wrongness of slavery. Grace caused him to repent.

The lavishness of God's grace was indeed amazing as far as Newton was concerned when he looked over the life he had lived and the healed man he'd become. The only way he could explain the change that had taken place in his life was to point to God's amazing grace.

Grace can turn your life right-side up.

What is this Grace spoken of? It is sheer delight in the wonder of it all.

Grace is like the little Japanese boy who had just had his chest cracked open and a new heart stuffed into the center of his being (something we all need in one way or another). He and I (who couldn't understand a word of each other's language) were there in front of a fireplace, popping popcorn and sharing the wonder of it together— there in front of us a mini big-bang of new creation going on, with butter and salt running down our elbows—both of glad to be alive— just like in the beginning. This is grace.

So what can we learn from all this?

1. It's okay to sing the blues—to God. Say, pray, sing, scream, write— anyway you want—but sing your blues unto the Lord.

2. We can dare to hope by remembering God's faithfulness—getting our antennae up for everyday grace and dusting for fingerprints.

3. At my worst—God is faithful, God is gracious—this is opposite of my tendencies. God is watching, peeking from the side curtain. He can't wait to bestow grace—especially when we sin. It's his goodness and kindness that lead us to repentance.

4. We need to learn the language of grace (Grace as a Second Language)—to thank our way out of the blues—not think, but thank our way out.

5. Our blues experiences are God's grace opportunities—the places where God most often shows up. Where you'll most find His fingerprints. Be ready.

God has come to us in these difficult days with words of grace, introducing the "yet" into our struggles with sorrow and hope, teaching us something of His language of grace—which casts out fear.

The lament of Jeremiah the blues singer has been my song:

"The water rose over my head, and I cried out, 'This is the end!'
But I called on your name, Lord, from deep within the pit.
You heard me when I cried, 'Listen to my pleading!
Hear my cry for help!'
Yes, you came when I called; you told me, 'Do not fear.'"[28]

Though I, like the author of Lamentations, struggle from the time I get up in the morning and throughout the day, every day I feel uplifted, held in the strong and gracious hands of God. And every day I am profoundly thankful for another day of grace. I hope you will be too.

"Yet, I still dare hope when I remember this:

The faithful love of the Lord never ends
His mercies never cease
They are new every morning
Great is Thy faithfulness

The Lord is my portion, my inheritance
Therefore I will hope in him."[29]

This is the language of Grace—as overheard in a blues club.

A Grain of Wheat
~6~

"Truly, truly, I say to you, unless a grain of wheat falls into the earth and dies, it remains alone; but if it dies, it bears much fruit." (Jesus)[30]

I've had a unique opportunity in the last fourteen years to observe families coming from Japan to UCLA Medical Center for heart transplants—new hearts. This occasion arose when my Japanese wife responded to a news picture that looked like our niece in Japan. This led her into a volunteer role, me into a supportive observer role, and our family into an incredible journey with A Grain of Wheat.

August 2001, Japan

Matsuo Basho, the old Japanese haiku poet master, invites us to see that life may be understood in the capturing, or framing, of a telling moment…

An old silent pond
Into the pond a frog jumps
Splash! Silence again [31]

Old Mt Fuji was there, visible behind the haze. We wove our way through flowers at the base of the mountain. Covered tricycles pedaled by couples coaxed a breeze out of the humid summer air.

And there, right in front of us (which is where most important things are found), little Riho and her papa pedaled, and smiled, a haiku moment framed. For there, in the smile, a story was being told across the miles and the years. I just happened to be listening.

Two and a half years earlier, a defective heart was discovered in this one so little. Plans were made to travel from Tokyo to UCLA. Financial obstacles soon arose, almost as big as Mt. Fuji. A half-million-dollar deposit would be required—a big ante in this real-life high-stakes gamble—a million or two when all was said and done—that could be done—for there were no guarantees.

Well, Papa Endo and Mama Endo and Riho, along with their cardiologist, Dr. Dodo (one of my favorite names, one of my favorite people), made their way to the USA.

My wife gathered ordinary folks, volunteers, to meet and greet and welcome; to translate and negotiate; to build bridges across different cultural assumptions and understanding—a net of support for this high-wire act. There was a network formed between doctors and nurses and financial offices; apartment and restaurant owners; TV producers and students and families—all of whom were previously strangers. And using all the human and medical resources available, they began to get ready—to wait—for a new heart.

All lessons previously learned were called forth and integrated into a life-or-death experience. All went to work with all of their hearts. And the wait went on, summoning all emotional and spiritual resources for such a time as this.

On her second day in the USA, little Riho—one and a half years old—went into cardiac arrest. She was attached to an artificial heart support machine—ECMO—but this could sustain her for only a limited time. The clock was ticking.

On the third day the longed-for call came, along with a helicopter and the ice chest which contained this strange thing called a heart—alive and beating. Donor and donee were both catching glimpses of a mystery that lies at the heart of the universe: someone's death can provide life for another. The exchanged life—my life for yours—it goes on all the time, sometimes even in our own hearts.

It was then that the noble ones swung into action. Dr. Hillel Laks and the UCLA staff rose in the middle of the night, ready to summon every lesson ever learned, every skill honed, every talent given. Timing is everything. But these brave men and women are also humble. The walk a very fine line: they must know when to risk and when not to. They must trust that their learning and experience will become wisdom in this moment. For they held this little one's life in their hands. They were holding our hearts as well.

Mr. and Mrs. Endo rushed Riho to the OR and the work began. The little chest was torn open; the old hard, shriveled heart detached; a scaffold of machines, tubes, and computers erected; and the new heart was inserted and connected. The bloody ribcage was closed. All eyes were on the machines and Riho—seeking signs of life. Those blips began to take shape, spelling out symbols of hope. New life had been formed—we had all been transformed.

Herein lies the metaphor.

"Thus saith the Lord, 'A new heart also will I give you… I will take out your stony, stubborn heart and give you a tender responsive heart.'"[32]

The weary nobility was done, for the time being, leaving the most courageous little one to now take up her own battle. And everyone was left wondering what just happened. Maybe most of all Dr. Laks, one of the best in the business, who humbly admitted that this was something beyond him, part of something much bigger—something at the heart of the universe—maybe even the very heart of God.

Meanwhile, back in Japan, many received the news with great joy, but a few had conflicting emotions. Mr. and Mrs. Monobe, who'd pioneered changes in Japanese transplant laws, celebrated—yet privately, for they must once again mourn the loss of their eight-year-old daughter, Miyuki, for want of a heart. Another family who had chronicled their heart-transplant drama in a popular book rejoiced, and yet wondered again why their three-year-old boy didn't receive a heart.

The "why" questions cloud the hearts of many, not least of all the donors' families, who must share their grief and gratitude anonymously. These are the hard lessons buried deep within the recesses of the human heart—and God's.

It was now two years later as my wife and I rode through those flowers at the base of Mt. Fuji, watching little Riho ride with her father up ahead of us. They'd invited us into their story, we tried to listen, and a framed moment had spoken—sounding a lot like God's promise of a new heart.

Heart Lessons

Heart is that place at the very center of our being—our core, essence. Heart is where deepest feelings are felt, important decisions are made—out of which our life's course is determined. Heart is the place through which relationships are created and sustained.

Sometimes our hearts become hard, stony, stubborn, rebellious. In Israel, hearts had become hard. God's people had turned away from God, broken covenant, replaced their Creator with created idols—thus disconnecting themselves from the very source of life. They were just living in the illusion of life-support. They needed a new heart. God was the only one who could do that operation. And he was willing. One greater than Dr. Laks is here.

How do I get a new heart?

1. I need to realize I need one—and I can't do the transplant myself. I must allow God to examine my heart and show me for who I re-

ally am—accept the biblical, prophetic diagnosis of my condition and admit that spiritually I will die without a new heart.

2. I need to ask for a new heart. Go to God, the source. Jesus said, "Which of you if your child asks you for a fish will give him a stone? How much more will your Father in heaven give the Holy Spirit (new heart) to those who ask? Trust God's promise: 'I will give you a new heart.'"

3. I need a donor (the hardest part for transplant patients is the wait). The good news is that we already have one. God has so loved us that He's given us His Son. Jesus' sacrifice reveals the heart of God for us: "This is my body broken—my blood poured out—for you." The Son of God is the ultimate donor—laying down his life for me and you—"My life for yours: My heart for yours."

4. I need to get on the table and submit to the operation. A heart transplant is a grueling operation of many hours. So it is with us. It often takes a while for God to put a new heart within us. Many times we are torn at the center of our being, but our Great Physician knows what He's doing. And the operation, as I understand the cross, has already been paid for.

"Thus saith the Lord, 'A new heart also will I give you... I will take out your stony, stubborn heart and give you a tender responsive heart.'"

How do we know if we have a new heart?

1. We feel alive. When Riho got a new heart she started crawling all over the place and talking. We become full of life; it's like being born—again.

2. We want to eat—our appetite comes back—skinny kids fatten up. Spiritually, new hearts hunger after God and the things of God.

We have a strong desire to feed upon God's Word and drink of God's Spirit.

3. We want to play—like Riho on the floor. We are free to live, free to play. Life becomes too serious to be taken seriously, and joy becomes our work, for "joy is the serious business of heaven." (C.S. Lewis)

4. New hearts are filled with gratitude for new life, forever grateful for our donor. This appreciation for life and sacrifice causes a deep joy within us.

5. With a new heart, life is somehow different—life is now lived on purpose. There's not a lot of time to waste. We make the most of each moment, each person, each opportunity. Every relationship is important. Life becomes sacramental—all ordinary things become more special, centered around the Giver of new hearts. There's a larger wonder at it all.

6. New hearts begin to do the things God created us for. We become much more concerned with God's will and ways. We become more careful and willing to obey God's commands. No longer "I have to" but rather, "I get to, and want to."

7. New hearts bear relational fruit: sacrificial love for one another, peace between and within, a deep inner joy independent of circumstances, and more (see Galatians 5).

"Truly, truly, I say to you, unless a grain of wheat falls into the earth and dies, it remains alone; but if it dies, it bears much fruit." (Jesus)

In both physical and spiritual heart transplants, we discover God's fingerprints are all over the place!

An Epiphany of Sorts
~7~

Have you ever had an epiphany? A revealing moment of something eternally significant? A divine "Aha" experience?

Epiphany is a time when we reflect on the journey of the Magi, or wise men, to Bethlehem. They had been seeking in many ways and for many days, and at the right time ventured out. Following a star, they inquired of the political and religious powers-that-be as to where the king of the Jews might be born; this led them to a baby born in a barn. They knelt before him in worship, presented their gifts, and then, being warned by an angel of the Lord regarding these same powers, they went home by another way.

Managua 1987

I went to Nicaragua to study the religious, political, social, and economic aspects of the so-called liberation movements in Central and South America for the intended purposes of understanding, communicating, and peacemaking. This was in the time of the Sandinista revolution and the Iran-Contra controversies.

In Managua we visited with the president's cabinet, met at the Secretary of Defense's home, conferred with the US ambassador, and met with religious and military officials and with news organizations on all different sides of the revolution. It was my first encounter with political propaganda—it came from all sides.

We heard triumphant accounts and horror stories of the ongoing revolution. The most memorable was in the small office of Violeta Chamorro, who told of her husband's torture by the Sandinistas. (She later became the president of Nicaragua.) We also learned of the thousands who were killed and impoverished in the name of revolution, along with destruction attributed to the U.S. and the Contra revolutionaries.

My epiphany came one night in the town of Esteli. We were brought to a motel to stay. Late at night we were led through town to the basement of a church where we were told the Contra (U.S.) side of things—gruesome stories of violence, torture, and murder. We went home under a full moon, seeing bullet-ridden buildings and watching rockets shoot through the sky nearby. When we arrived back at the motel, the parking lot was filled with Cuban, Russian, and East German military vehicles: trucks, tanks, and missile launchers.

It was difficult to sleep that night with all these things going on in my head. I had finally gotten to sleep when I was suddenly awakened to the most God-awful screams and noises. We heard pounding on the doors and horrible sounds from the streets right in front of us. I could only envision people being dragged away to be tortured. My mother was right. I was a fool to be in such a place.

My roommate and I were both scared spitless—and we thought this was our night to die. I went into the bathroom to see if there was a back way out. I found a window, with the continuing horrible sounds just beyond it. I was able to get it open and there I found the source of all the commotion. The barnyard animals were waking up! Roosters and pigs and cows were raising an early morning ruckus and the sounds were echoing all around us. The soldiers were merely being wakened for morning maneuvers. But the political climate and fears of the night before had so stoked my imagination that I thought it was surely the end.

This story, I believe, is a microcosm of some of what is going on in our world, our country, our homes, our church, and our very selves. It is an epiphany of sorts.

We all have conflicts and wounds—some real, some imagined. Fears can be paralyzing and captivating, robbing us of life and hope and faith. Some are very real—abandonment, betrayal, violation, terrorism, cancer, loss, death—and some are just barnyard illusions. We need help sorting them out.

Into this fearful world someone struck a match 2,000 years ago. Some read the wisdom of ancient Hebrew prophets, while others read the configuration of stars for signs of God. And as they compared notes, they decided to head out, leaving eastern lands, following the lights they were given. They landed in another barnyard, this one in Bethlehem. They'd remembered to bring gifts along, which just so happened to fit the descriptions described by Isaiah many years before.

There they found a teenage mother and her husband with an ordinary human baby, though they sensed something extraordinary was going on—a king, they believed, a light, they hoped, healing of a kind—and there they knelt and worshiped. An epiphany of sorts.

Maybe this is just what we need.

As I look back on the past few years, reading and reflecting on my journal and the events that have taken place—my dad recovering from a stroke, my wife's cancer, pain in our son's life, the death of my father-in-law, some disappointments and losses of friends—it's been hard. But in reflection, and especially in conversation with my wife at breakfast, there has been some light in our darkness, some hope in our fears, some healing in broken places, some upholding when we were weak and weary, some faithful folks caring—all of it redeeming, in an epiphany of sorts.

As we look forward, Eepiphanies past and present (God's fingerprints) point me in some directions I hope we might travel together.

1. **Epiphanies call me to follow the lead of the wise men and seek the Lord more intentionally.** To deepen the relationship. To bend my knee in places where I've resisted. To consider more purposefully the gifts I bring to Him, and those I offer in His name.

2. **Like the wise men, I am hearing a word in the epiphany to not listen to the intimidating powers in my life.** This past year, in the valley of the shadow of death, I have continually heard the words "Fear not." I am being called to listen to God's Word above all others, to fear Him alone (for this is the beginning of wisdom), to kneel before King Jesus only, and to go home by another way if necessary.

3. **Epiphany is about relationships.** With God and with each another—for this God sent his Son into our world. For me it means a greater valuing and cherishing of relationships I am given. This means that I choose to make the most of each moment and person—realizing life is a gift, life is fragile, life is precious.

Epiphany for me means I am to have honest discussions and listen deeply and carefully, especially to people with whom I differ; that I respect each person and have greater confidence in the truth by seeking accurate information before I blame or accuse, distance or disconnect, estrange or alienate. How we do relationships is part of worshiping the King.

In days ahead, let's build a fire around which we can gather and be warmed and see each other face-to-face and have humble conversations. Let's keep the fire in the fireplace, and with grace, humility, and wisdom keep it from burning down the house—or like the town of Esteli, which was destroyed soon after my visit.

4. **In the epiphany I am called to a higher vision**. To allow the epiphany of the Jesus Story-Christ event to shape within me a higher vision for life. Our world is being torn apart by culture wars and polarized by socioeconomic agendas of left, right, and everywhere in between. As Christians, if we merely mirror the anger, fears, and discord of the world, we as people of God have nothing to say of hope to the world, no healing to offer, no light to bring upon the needs of our lonely world.

Without a higher vision, we have no epiphany to offer. I am determined to not let any barnyard animals scare me into a lower vision, but to aim for Christ's higher vision. How about you?

In the first century, Jesus had several political, social, and religious options available to Him, each with their own agendas being promoted as the will of God. There were the conservative Pharisees, the liberal Sadducees, the radically violent Zealots, and the Essenes, who withdrew to the desert. But Jesus had a different vision, a higher vision. He called it the Kingdom of God, and He called us to seek that Kingdom first.

John 13 says this is something of what it looked like: "Jesus, knowing he had come from God and was going to God, took up a towel and basin and washed his disciples' feet." Jesus knew who He was and where He'd come from and where He was going; therefore, he chose to be servant of all—essential in His Kingdom.

Now, among those early disciples was Simon the Zealot and Matthew the tax collector, who traditionally would have hated each other's guts. Clarence Jordan (NT Greek scholar and southern farmer) said that there must have been many a night when Jesus had to sleep between Simon and Matthew. Epiphany means I'm going to try to let him do so between me and those with whom I significantly differ. We are called to relate to one another as if Christ were always between us—because He always is.

If we see our identity as primarily "in Christ" (versus in a political side or social cause), then we will know where we've come from and where we're going, and we'll pick up a towel and basin and wash one another's feet along the way. We must remember that it is God's world and Christ's church—not mine or yours—and He will build it. We can trust Him. It's an epiphany of sorts.

5. **It's true we do have legitimate differences: The question is how we will treat each other when we differ.** It's important to hold our own convictions and to honor our consciences before God. It's also important to respect the consciences and convictions of others. As C.S. Lewis tells us: We can meet in the common hallway of the many diverse rooms of the Christian household (*Mere Christianity*).

6. **It's not enough to have epiphanies or New Year's resolutions. We need the power to carry them out.** Gordon Cosby (Church of the Savior) helps me in this regard: *"There is an essential quality of life, different from that of the truly human and transcending it. There is a whole new realm of power that was released in the Resurrection and which broke into human life at Pentecost. This power can flow into our lives. We are in a new realm."*[33]

7. **We are all invited to the Lord's table—a place of prime epiphany.** All are welcome. It's a big tent. We don't have to agree on social issues, politics, or ways of being church—only that Jesus is the Lord, the head of the body, the host of the table—and we who have gathered in His name are His Body. As one of my professors at UCLA says, "Jesus would eat with anyone who would eat with him" (S. Scott Bartchy). Christians should be willing to do the same. We are invited to the table to be in fellowship and com-

munion with people with whom we differ. It is Christ who is our unity. He is what we have in common.

Now, it's time to head back to the barn.

In the midst of the conflicts and challenges we all face, in our days ahead let epiphany shed some light on our relationships of all kinds. Let's not let the barnyard animals of fear distort, distance, or demonize people with whom we differ. Mature love casts out fear—let it. Jesus is calling us all on to a higher vision, that of the Kingdom of God. Allow God's spirit to empower and lead you to the barnyard wherein is born the Servant King. And while you kneel to worship, pick up a towel and basin, and start washing dirty feet.

It's an epiphany of sorts!

Sam's Club
~8~

One day a post-hole digger, a professor who'd gotten his PhD in theology, philosophy and hubris from the University of Jerusalem, stood up to test Jesus by asking Him a question (puffin' on a pipe, lookin' wise): *"Teacher, what should I do to inherit eternal life?"* [33]

Jesus (blowing a bubble with some gum a kid had given Him) replied, *"What does the law of Moses (the Torah) say? How do you read it?"* (This sends him back to the professor's area of expertise, as He often does with us.)

Professor: *"You must love the Lord your God with all your heart, all your soul, all your strength, and all your mind. And love your neighbor as yourself."*

Jesus: *"Right!"* (doing his best Groucho Marx imitation, "Get this man a kewpie doll!") *"Do this and you will live."*

But the professor wanted to justify his actions (he was probably writing a grant), so he asked Jesus, *"And who is my neighbor?"*

And Jesus replied with a story:

A man was traveling on a business trip from downtown LA up to the Trump Resort in Palos Verdes. As he was driving up Hawthorne Boulevard, he was carjacked by some gangsters. They stripped him of his Lakers jacket and brand-new Nikes. They beat him up, drove away with his Lexus, and left him half dead beside the road.

By coincidence a minister came along on his way to a golf game. But when he saw the man lying there, he crossed to the other side of the road and passed him by. (In his religion, touching the dead was considered impure, and even more importantly, he might miss his tee time.)

Soon after, an associate minister drove by. He stopped, did a lookie-loo at the man lying there, but he had a Board of Christian Mission meeting to go to, so he also passed on by the other side.

Then a despised Samaritan came along. We'll call him Sam. (Jews had no dealings with these half-breed folks; Sam wasn't our kind of people. You can fill in what kind of person that is for you.) When he saw the man, he felt compassion for him. Going over to him, Sam soothed his wounds with olive oil and used some wine as a disinfectant and bandaged the man's wounds.

Then he put the man in his own car, an old Pinto, and took him down to the Holiday Inn, where he took care of him. The next day Sam handed the hotel manager a few hundred bucks, saying: "Please take care of this man. If his bill runs higher than this, put it on my Visa."

Jesus then, reframing the original question, said to the professor: *"Now which of these three would you say was a neighbor to the man who was robbed, beaten, and wounded?"*

Professor (whose pipe had now gone out) said: *"The one who showed him compassion."*

Jesus: *"Yes—now go and do the same."*

Here's our invitation to join Sam's club. Notice what's involved:

1. Sam *saw* the man. Compassion sees the person, and the person is what matters.

2. Sam *felt* compassion for the man. He imagined into the man's situation and pain and felt something of what it must be like. Compassion gets in the other's shoes and walks around for a while.

3. Sam *went over to* him. Compassion meets the person where they are, at their point of need. Compassion translates seeing and feeling into ***doing***, gets involved—hands on, up close, not from a distance, neither from above.

4. Sam *soothed* his wounds, *cleaned* them, and *bandaged* them. Compassion brings a gentle touch, a soothing voice, is attentive to the wounded person.

5. Sam put the man *in his own* car. Compassion is not afraid to get dirty. In Sam's club what we have has been given is to be used for the sake of others.

6. Sam *took him* to the hotel and *took care* of him. Compassion gets people to a safe place and sees the caring through as far as possible.

7. Sam *paid for* the man's expenses, whatever was needed. Compassion is willing to spend itself for the person in need.

Summary: Sam loved his neighbor as he would have loved himself.
(And therefore God's fingerprints were all over it!)

Notice how Jesus reframed the question:

The professor asked, *"Who is my neighbor?"* hoping to justify his already narrow definition of neighbor (i.e., me and my own—family, friends, nation, color, etc.).

Jesus turns the question around: *"Who are you a neighbor to?"* hoping to make the definition of neighbor limitless.

This is the question posed to us: *Who am I a neighbor to?*

Notice how Jesus appeals to what the man already knows:

"What does the Torah say?" (his area of expertise) "How do you read it?"

The professor knew the right answers, but he was failing the real-life test.

Jesus: "You are right. Do this and you will experience an eternal quality of life."

This is the challenge presented to us: Do what you already know about loving God and loving your neighbor. We don't need more knowledge; we need more doing of what we already know. Do this and you will live.

Compassion can be in smaller, less heroic things:
- A cup of coffee and listening with your ears, eyes, and heart
- A phone call to let the person know you see and feel some of their loss
- Being with a person quietly when life is dark or lonely
- Praying for the wounds and loss

Compassion needs to travel with wisdom
We are not saviors; God is. We are not here to rescue people from their own inner work. We just come to see and feel and respond in some way to a need. It's a small thing, to be approached with humility.

1. **There is a difference between helping and meddling**

Meddling is the opposite of helpfulness because it is forcing your-self into another person's life. To meddle is to violate the other's sacred choice. Compassion opens one's self as a refuge to the other and respects their choices.

2. **It's okay to say no in order to say yes**
   Jesus did not respond to every need or demand—He focused on what He was called to do. So it should be with us: Focus on what's clear: Do one or two things well. You are not called to do everything. If you say yes to too many things, you're probably saying no to priority things. If you trip over an obvious need, it's probably a call to compassion. Or if something has been continu-ally tugging on your heart for a long time, take a step and see.

3. **Compassion burn-out**
   This happens when you try to do too many things, or for too long. You might need a rest, a break, a Sabbath. Maybe you need to get some sleep or take a day off regularly. Like Mary (Luke 10) maybe you need some time to just sit at the feet of Jesus, time-out from busyness (like Martha), and let God restore your soul beside the still waters.

4. **The wounded neighbor might be right in front of you,** living in your house, or working near you, living right next to you, or sitting in church beside you. These are primary calls to compassion—the neighbors we come across.

5. **You might feel like you are the person in the ditch,** wounded, beaten up by life, robbed, cheated, hurt—half alive, half dead. The author of Sam's story does what He teaches. Jesus sees you and feels your pain. He comes to where you are—it doesn't mat-ter how you got there. He comes to soothe and to wrap your wounds. He's given up all he possessed to care for you—laying down His life for you. He calls you friend. And he wants to bring

you into a safe place, entrust you into the care of some other wounded healers. He is the author of wise compassion.

Invitation: If you'd like to join Sam's club, you're invited. Here are the requirements. Please repeat after me:

- I will try to keep my eyes open for persons in need, in pain, wounded.
- I will try to feel some of what they must feel.
- I will act on what I see and feel—I will do something about it.
- I will go to where that person is—meet them where they are—at their point of need.
- I will learn skills in soothing wounds and healing hurt people.
- I will make the resources God has given me available to the needs of my neighbors.
- I will try to bring that person into a safe and caring place.
- I will follow through on the care I begin.

To the best of my ability, by God's sufficient gtace.

Welcome to Sam's Club!

The Lion Lady
~ 9 ~

"When I was young I admired clever people. Now that I am old, I admire kind people." Rabbi Abraham Joshua Heschel

The call came about 10:45 on a Sunday eve. As a young minister in a small town, I had had a tiring day. It was my custom to gear down on Sunday evenings by watching some mindless TV show until I fell asleep. That night it was the return of *Gilligan's Island.*

When the phone rang, a lady was crying, talking incoherently, but wanting me to visit her—that night. (I thought, *Now I'll never know if Gilligan got off the island.*) I took down the address, which was eight miles out of town in the desert oil fields. Using pastoral precaution, I asked my wife at the time to go with me. By the time we got to the house, it was after midnight.

I saw a high white board fence surrounding the property of what looked like a trailer home. There were many trees and bushes all around and a large sign that I got out to read: "Keep Out—or be shoot!" (I realized I was not dealing with a person familiar with English's past tense.) Before I knew it there was a woman standing in front of me: white tee-shirt, bell-bottom jeans, long black hair, with matching blackened teeth and a belt with bullets in it. "Come on in," she said, eyeing me warily. (And this was my second mistake; the first was being there in the first place.)

She led us around to the back where there were many abandoned cars and trucks. We were ushered into the back gate, where I met a donkey and a llama. Guided by a path we headed for the back door. Two angry dogs were tied to trees on either side of the path, with just enough room for us to get by. Behind one tree were two large cages, which I later found to contain lions.

We entered the trailer and she offered us a seat upon a sofa that was obviously purchased from a corner gas station, along with the velvet paintings of Elvis on the wall. We sank into the sofa as the woman took a chair directly in front of me. There were five or six large bird-cages around the living room with several exotic birds making quite a racket.

I felt as if I were on trial as the woman began to harangue me with the many injustices of the world, while knocking down screwdrivers like they were going out of style.

I made my third mistake when I tried to bring God into the picture. "God!" she yelled. "God is cruel. God killed Elvis, who was the love of my life. God kills all of his servants—look at Moses. Don't tell me about God." And by then she was screaming in my face. It was then when I began to see the headlines in the next day's paper. It was the stuff of which axe-murder movies were made.

She sat back down, which was when I noticed a goat looking at me through the front slider-door. Just as I was trying to figure out an escape, a mouse ran across the kitchen tile, and a cat leaped out of nowhere, caught the mouse, and carried it in its mouth—despite two crippled back legs. Which is when I learned the cat, and many other animals in this place, had been rescued after being hit on the highway.

This was getting weirder by the minute. Then I smelled something awful. "Brutus!" she yelled and opened the door to a bedroom. Out came one of the biggest dogs I'd ever seen. He walked over and looked down on me sitting on that sofa. "Sit!" she ordered. I did. She meant the dog. And I knew then and there she was in control of the whole scene.

At that moment, the lady got up and went to the fridge to fix another screwdriver, and my wife got up and sat next to her at the kitchen table. The woman began to cry; my ex-wife listened, sympathized, held her hand, spoke softly, and cried with her. *And this turned the situation.* Eventually we found out her husband had taken two lion cubs to town because they were sick. The vet was closed, so he took them to the hospital's emergency room. But some policemen noticed the lions and cited the man with a ticket. When he argued with them, he was taken to jail. And this, among many other things, is what had caused all the ruckus. Well, needless to say we got out alive and I learned something about kindness.

There is a fitting Japanese proverb to this story:

> *"One kind word can warm three winter months."*

Kindness made the difference. Kindness could even tame a lion lady. There was wisdom in this kindness.

Kindness is a way of:

1. Listening. Listening carefully, from the humility of a position below. Seeking to stand under in order to understand. Kindness listens in a way we like to be listened to: attentive, valued, understood—with both eyes, both ears, faced toward the other person, off with the game, put the cell phone down. Kindness is being fully present in listening to another.

2. Speaking. Speaking in a mellowed-cheese, fine-wine kind of voice—bringing truth, yet it is a truth aged by kindness. It's often not what you say, but how you say it. "The tongue of the wise (and the kind) bring forth healing."[34]

3. Affirming another person and encouraging their gifts. *You* are important, *you* are significant, *you* matter to me. Your gifts and thoughts and efforts are valued and welcomed. I need them. I need you. This is kindness.

4. Bringing comfort or courage as needed. It is the held hand in the chemo ward, the sitting next to in the emergency room. It is the walk alongside another through valleys of shadow of death. It is being with and for the other, speaking or acting the fitting word with truth and grace: a word to soothe or a word to strengthen.

5. Helping someone at their point of need –coming alongside and taking the next step together. It means not imposing my idea of what the need is, but listening well enough to know the real need—and then meeting it. (See Sam's Club.)

Kindness, at its root, is how we treat those who are "our kind"—folks like us, our family (kin), our friends, or the flock we fly with—people with whom we share something in common, people we treat as our kind as we do our own selves. There is kindness toward our kind.

But the Word of God calls us to something higher and deeper—when we find a way to make someone different as "our kind," this is one of God's ideas of kindness.

God's Kindness

"We have tasted God's kindness," says St. Peter. And in so doing we detect His fingerprints:

Kind in creation, gifting us His image. Though we are different (God vs. human) we are made to be His kind, treated like kin. With God there is the kindness of welcome, food and drink, conversation, creativity, generosity, and partnership.

Even when we mess up and alienate ourselves from God, we are treated with kindness: Just as in the garden, fig leaves are made to cover our shame, and on a cross sacrifice was made to atone for our failures. God, in Jesus, is with us and for us.

In this strange event called Incarnation, God becomes human, to be one of us, one of our kind. And though we treat Him as not one of our kind, God kindly pursues us in grace, suffers what we suffer, dies bearing our sin, and raises us in the power of resurrection to reclaim us as His kind. We have tasted God's kindness.

We can learn this wisdom of kindness.
"Be ye kind one to another..." (St. Paul to the Ephesians)

There are random acts of kindness, which are good, and there are intentional acts that are even better. Intentional acts of kindness make kindness a lifestyle. So, where do we begin?

Take a step:

1. **Ask the Lord to show you someone in need of kindness.** Who pops into your mind? If someone comes to mind, ask God for a way to be kind to that person. If you are willing, He will help. When something becomes clear—do it, no matter how small. Take the step.

2. **Make a list and check it twice.** Invite the Spirit of God to examine your speech and actions for harsh edges. This might come in a still moment, through another person, or in the middle of a shower. When those hard edges are shown to you, ask God to soften those edges. Ask the Lord to tenderize your heart—like a good steak, mellowed cheese, or aged wine. "Lord, please season my words with grace and may my actions be in the wisdom of kindness."

Cooperate with God's spirit that He might bring forth the fruit of kindness in your life.

3. **Take someone different** (in culture, politics, religion, or values) **out for coffee or lunch.** Listen to their story, listen very carefully, imagine their life and the view from which they see things. Remember that everyone you meet is afraid of something, loves something, and has lost something. Everyone you meet is fighting a hard battle of their own. Try to make that person one of your own kind—not by argument—but by kindness (the way God is toward you). *"It is the goodness and kindness of God that leads us to turn, to change, to repent."(Romans 2:4)*

4. **Take some of the coal out of your stocking.** Get rid of the grouch and Grinch, the critical spirit that needs so desperately to show people where they are wrong or defective or lacking. Do a gift exchange: Instead put on a mask of kindness—you might just grow into it. When I put on a Santa Claus suit, I find I grow into it, becoming more jolly, merry, and kind. "Fake it till you make it." Leave some fingerprints.

5. **Think of someone difficult in your life.** It shouldn't be hard. Someone who has hurt you or offended you (or whom you took up an offense toward)—a personal enemy. **Determine to bless them in some kind way**: a card, a note, an email. Pray for them. Give them (and yourself) the gift of forgiveness (release them, let go of whatever it is)—just as God in Christ has kindly forgiven you.

6. **Offer a cup of cold water** (or coffee), a phone call of appreciation, bring someone who is alone some cookies and sit a while to share a few, bring some clothes or blankets or food to a shelter and stay for lunch and some conversation, anonymously send help to someone who has been affected by economic, job, or

health needs. Partner with some fellow entrepreneurs to create a new job and drop it into someone's life.

7. **Do something extravagant, audacious, unheard of—blow somebody's mind**—but do it silently, secretly. "Be kind enough to yourself, not just to play it safe, but spend at least part of your lives like drunken sailors. For God's sake be extravagantly kind."[35]

There is wisdom in kindness—it can even tame lion ladies, so...

"Be as kind as you can
By all the means you can
In all the ways you can
In all the places you can
At all the times you can
To all the people you can
As long as you can."

(John Wesley)

"Be kind to one another, tenderhearted,
forgiving one another as God in Christ has forgiven you."[36]

The Dawn of the Remarkable
(All Things New)
~10~

"A fiery horse with the speed of light, a cloud of dust and a hearty 'Hi-yo, Silver!'" The Lone Ranger, a man of disguise coming into town to bring justice and to turn wrong into right. When he had finished his work, someone would ask, "Who was that masked man?" They would discover a silver bullet on the table—this was the Lone Ranger's signature, his fingerprint. It meant he had been there and done that. And then came the response: "Why, he's the Lone Ranger!"

This morning we rise to hear the stories again of Jesus and His resurrection. In our day, we sometimes have difficulty recognizing His risen presence. The stories in the gospels give us some clues as to how He might show up. Like kids on an Easter Egg hunt, we look for silver bullets (fingerprints), for they will lead us toward the dawn of a remarkable thing.

Maggie
"Men!" She was a woman with a past. She knew men—the dark sides of men, the weak sides. Her past had twisted her soul with torment and fear (and she felt unclean); she trusted no one, especially men—until she met a different man. This man knew all about her, and with mercy and grace began to free her of torment and fear, shame and guilt. She began to feel free and clean. And with humble gratitude she began to follow him wherever he went and learned from him a new way to live. She began to form friendships with others who had joined him. And they became like family, only a different kind

of family—one with hope. There were women, and there were men. And now that Jesus had died that terrible death, the hope was gone. The leader was gone. Who would hold the family together now? Not the men, who were home cowering in fear behind closed doors. As soon as their bacon was near the frying pan, they sold Jesus out in a Brooklyn minute. Men!

Well, it was nearing dawn and Mary Magdalene headed down the back streets of Jerusalem (she knew them all too well) toward the Garden Tombs. With all the commotion of the last couple of days, there were some last- minute burial details to attend to. When she got to the gravesite, she found the covering stone had been rolled away. She fearfully peeked in and saw a young man in a shiny white robe sitting on the right side. She was stunned. But the messenger said, "Don't be afraid. You're looking for Jesus, right? The one who was crucified? He's not here. He is risen. Go and tell the disciples he's gone to Galilee to meet up." She ran like the wind, heart pounding, into town—half scared, half out of her mind with wild joy. She ran up the stairs and started banging on the door to the upper room.

Johnny and Pete

No one answered the door right away; they were too busy arguing. "What went wrong?"

"Judas, that's what. Traitor. He ruined the whole thing. What are we going to do now? They'll be coming after us soon."

Pete was staring out the window, replaying recent events, flinching inside as he beat himself up over having denied Jesus. Cringing as he regretted his bold words of loyalty a few weeks before. Now all he could hear was that Rooster mocking his cowardice—over and over again.

"Shhh! Someone's at the door." They were afraid to answer it. Mary pounded louder, yelling something they couldn't quite understand. Someone opened the door and Mary tumbled in out of breath. "He's not there. He's risen! He's going to meet us in Galilee."

"Poor woman." They regarded her with pity. Thought it was nonsense. But Pete ran out the door, Johnny right behind him. Always in competition, they raced each other to the tomb. But when they looked in, they saw empty linen wrappings. They went home again, wondering what had happened. Each had their own crisis of faith swirling around within them. Mary stayed by the tomb.

And the Gardener whispered, "Mary," thus leaving her His fingerprint.

Tommy

When they got back to the upper room, they locked themselves in for fear. Suddenly, Jesus was standing there among them. He didn't even knock. To disciples trembling with fear and astonishment, He simply said, "Peace!" And then He showed them His wounds in His wrists and the side near his heart. And then the place exploded with joy— they were partying like five-year-olds when hope arrives.

Again He said, "Peace," and gave them a job to do. He sent them to do what the Father sent Him to do. Gave them a dose of the Holy Spirit to help and then called them to forgive anyone's sins. In other words, "Go proclaim Good News."

But Thomas wasn't there. He was probably home reading philosophy books, figuring out what he should do next. The disciples came spilling into his room, yelling, "We've seen the Lord!"

Tommy, who was born in Brooklyn, said, "I won't believe it till I see it. Unless I see the wounds and put my fingers into them." Eight days later, Jesus was just setting the bait. Tommy was with the others; again the doors were locked, again there was fear—it had been a week since they saw Jesus, and they were all doubting their own eyes and thinking a bit like Tom. And then Jesus was standing there—right in the middle of them.

"Peace." He looked at Thomas (with a look of amusement?) and said, "Put your finger here and look at my hands. Put your hand into the wound in my side. Believe it, Thomas."

Ol' Tommy just fell to his knees, and all he had to say was "My Lord and my God!"

If you're trying to hear this news of a remarkable thing, but find yourself on the Brooklyn side of skepticism, maybe you could try what Thomas did: Go take a look at Jesus' wounds. He says if we do something to the least of these (wounded, hungry, naked, imprisoned, broken, lonely), we do it to Him. Give it a try. Go touch the wounds of another, offer what you have as if it were Jesus. You might just find Him alive and the Lord of remarkable things.

(Fast-forward sixty years. John is in prison on the island of Patmos.)

All Things Made New

They call me John, and so I am. I'm getting up there in years, ninety-five or thereabouts. I've been spending my retirement years here on the Island of Patmos—not by choice. I've been exiled because of my allegiance to the one who has laid down His life for me, and whom I saw rise from the dead with my very own eyes.

I sit in my cell, day after day, looking over the sea to Asia Minor, where lie seven churches of which I was the pastor. I've been very concerned for my little flocks—for all flocks, for that matter. They, too, have made their stands in the face of the powers that be, daring to call Jesus Lord, not Caesar, not the Roman Empire. Consequently, some, like me, have paid for it. Some have lost loved ones, some have lost jobs, some have lost their lives, some have lost their faith. I wish I could comfort them, encourage them.

One day, looking through the bars I saw something. It was like heaven opened, right above those little churches, and I caught a glimpse of most wonderful things.

There was a kaleidoscope of images, not unlike Picasso or Chagall. Some had connections to the old Hebrew prophets, some were unlike anything I've seen. It has been hard to find words to describe these revelations.

I saw a throne in the midst of all the world's chaos. And there was One walking in the midst of the churches. I was scared to death. But He said, "Don't be afraid… I am the living one. I died, but look—I am alive forever. I hold the keys to death and the grave." Together these images seemed to say, "No matter how difficult it all seems, I am still on the throne. I am at work in the midst of the churches' challenges. Fear not! I have conquered the ultimate enemy, death. And I am alive making all things new."[37]

And then there were scrolls opening and trumpets blaring and bowls being poured out and beasts and serpents. Together they seemed to be a glimpse behind the scenes, giving shape to history, carving meaning out of our stories. And the future seemed to be breaking into the present—evoked by the prayers of God's People: "Thy kingdom come, thy will be done on Earth as it is in Heaven." The resurrected living Christ was injecting new life into creation.

I then saw a large multitude gathering around a beautiful table. It was a feast of some kind—a combination of the best reunions and wedding receptions to which you've ever been. We were all startled—with fear and wonder—at the roar of a lion. It came from the host's seat. But when I turned around, I saw a lamb—with visible wounds.

The Lion-Lamb invited creation to the feast—one by one. Each came to greet the host and bowed with deep reverence and awe. And as they found their seats around the table, friends began to recognize friends. And enemies became friends. Families were being reunited. And those with no family became one. Newness was being injected into creation.

As a widow walked away from greeting the host, she found the husband she'd lost to cancer. He was vibrant with life, a newer version, and kinder. They walked hand in hand. And the Lion's heart purred.

An elderly man with Alzheimer's was standing in line when he suddenly recognized the host. "I remember you!" he said, now all things coming clear. The host, with a gleam in His eye, said, "Welcome, young man! Now, here are some folks you might remember." And his wife and children came forward. And with a great laugh, the Lion joined their hands and said, "Do this, in remembrance of me." And they did.

Next came a mother now aged greatly—for she had lost her dear son when he was young. She came with head bowed before the host, who quickly said, "What's new?" She was greatly puzzled—until the Lamb pointed and said, "Woman, behold your son; son, behold your mother." And the woman seemed to grow younger as she looked into her son's eyes with wonder.

And so it went on and on—for "blessed are all who are invited to the Wedding feast of the Lamb."[38]

The curtain was pulled back once more...

Then I saw a new heaven and a new earth, for the old heaven and the old earth had disappeared. And the sea was also gone... I heard a loud shout from the throne, saying, "Look, God's home is now among his people! He will live with them, and they will be his people. God himself will be with them. He will wipe every tear from their eyes, and there will be no more death or sorrow or crying or pain. All these things are gone forever."

And the one sitting on the throne said, "Look, I am making everything new!" And then he said to me, "Write this down, for what I tell you is trustworthy and true." And he also said, "It is finished! I am the Alpha and the Omega—the Beginning and the End. To all who are thirsty I will give freely from the springs of the water of life. All who are victorious will inherit all these blessings, and I will be their God, and they will be my children."[39]

And so we come to hear the stories again of Jesus and His resurrection. In our day, we sometimes have difficulty recognizing His risen presence. The stories in the gospels give us some clues as to how He might show up. Like the kids on an Easter Egg hunt, we look for fingerprints, for they will lead us toward the dawn of a remarkable thing—where all things are made new!

Listening to the Story
~ 11 ~

There is a Story in our midst—stories within the Story, or Story within stories, or both. They invite, even seem to write my story. I see myself in the Story, the world through it, God in and beyond it—though most times darkly. I find hope and meaning and questions—and I question the hope and meaning—and find hope and meaning in the questioning. I find a framework for living and working, relating and thinking, sinning and saving, and praying and doubting. I see psalms and blues and screams and dreams and different hues of jazz refrains—I feel the poetic pushing me out beyond the safe places and into the land of the living.

It was in the cold of winter and we were waiting for the call. My uncle and aunt lived on the Passaic River just a few blocks from my house. Uncle Don had a measuring pole stuck in the river to see when the ice was thick enough, safe enough for us to ice skate. The call finally came and all the family—cousins and aunts and uncles and grandparents— came. Unk had rigged up speakers and lights in his backyard on the bank of the river so we could skate and listen to music at night. We'd skate up the river to my grandma's house about four blocks away, where Nan would wave and watch us for a while, and then we'd head back down the river to Aunt Pat and Uncle Don's. Young and old skated and everybody had a good time. When we got too tired or cold, we headed up the riverbank into the warm house, where a fire was blazing in the rock fireplace. The kids had hot chocolate with marshmallows and the grown-ups something warmer while we gathered around the fireplace. And that's when the stories began...

There are others gathered around the fire with us. We have other cousins, aunts and uncles, and grandparents, and in the holy day season, we gather around their stories.

Cousin Mary, a teenager, begins: "One night, I was alone, and a stranger came to my room. I was scared. 'Howdy, young lady. The Lord is with you, and you are favored among all women.' Now this was very disturbing; and I sensed he had something up his sleeve. Reading my pounding heart, he said, 'Fear not!' And then he said I would soon be pregnant. 'Fear not?' I said. 'Whaddya, nuts?' 'No, I'm Gabe and I bring a real-time message to you from God. You will bring forth a son and name him Joshua. He will be the Son of the Most High, sit on the throne of his great-great granddaddy King David, and of his kingdom there will be no end.' Then I said, 'Is this *Candid Camera*? Who are you really? How shall this be?' And the messenger said, 'God's Holy Presence will come upon you, overshadow you, and this holy one born of you shall be called Son of God.'"

At this point, cousin Mary shot a glance at her cousin Lizzie. The doctors had told Elizabeth she could not have children. But, here she was, six months pregnant. As Mary listened to the stories of the angel and gazed at Elizabeth, she began to understand. "Nothing is impossible with God."

Seems like sometimes God tips us off; sometimes God prepares us for what's ahead; sometimes God just leaves fingerprints. It's important to listen carefully.

Mary continued the story: "I was so confused in those days, and then came the belly bump—and then I was really scared. But I remembered the words of God—pondered them in my heart—of how and who and what to name him."

Then she looked at her husband, Joe, who had been very quiet, sipping one of Aunt Peggy's hot toddies. He was listening carefully to the story. He was listening to his own story. His face told that he'd caught a glimpse that it was all God's story.

Mary said, "Joseph was so kind, such a decent man. He found a safe place for us. He stuck with me, in spite of his doubts. He stayed with me, through it all. He believed me. He believed God." And so, he did.

"Zach and Lizzie were a great help to me in those days" (to which they both nodded humbly). "Being an unwed teenage girl was very difficult. But I remembered the angel's words and Joseph's faithfulness, and my cousins' kindness. And then I sang a song that became a hit.[40] I only intended to tell my story and how God was in it and to magnify Him.

"Well, there was no stork, no Santa, just pain and the baby came and we wrapped him in swaddling clothes, posed a few minutes for a manger photo for our first family Christmas card, and we named him Yeshua (Joshua)—'God saves'—for he would save his people from their sins."

And He did, and He does, and He will.

About that time old Uncle Simeon broke into the story: "I had been waiting a long time for God's promised One to come. One day He whispered into my soul that I would not die until I had seen the Messiah. That same whisper led me to the temple the other day and there Mary and Joseph were presenting little Josh to the Lord. They let me hold him and I thought, 'Now I can die in peace: I've seen the Lord's promise and salvation—this one would reveal God to all kinds of people.' I told young Mary that this child would be a joy to many, but many would also oppose him. And then I heard another of those silent whispers. I wanted to bite my tongue but couldn't and said quietly to her: 'And a sword shall pierce your very soul.'"

And it did, thirty-three years later.

Now, Aunt Anna, eighty-four years old, picked up the story from there. "In those days I stayed mostly in the temple to worship, fast, and pray. I saw Simeon speaking with Mary and Joseph that day—and I began praising God. And I just couldn't keep quiet, you know how it is—I was telling everyone who'd been waiting for God to rescue His people about this child. Yes, indeed. 'This is the One!' That's my story—and I'm stickin' to it."

I noticed a rough-looking character standing, leaning on the wall. He smelled a little funny—like sheep dip. He spoke up, saying, "Me and my homeboys was sittin' by the fire one night. Was colder than hell frozen over and the stars were close. We was cookin' up some mutton stew. Then this dude slipped into camp without our notice and cousin Joey says, 'How you doin'?' and the shiny dude says, 'How you doin'?' And then he says, 'Fear not. Something's happenin' over in the next town. I want you guys to head over there and check it out. I know that no one believes shepherd stories, but that's okay, God just wants you to know you're in the story, too. He wants you to meet the Good Shepherd. He wants to make you to lie down in green pastures, come beside still waters, restore your soul—just like the Song,[41] you know.'

"So we thought, what the hell—we could use some soul restoration, so we doused the fire, secured the sheep, and headed over to a barn in Bethlehem. We saw what was happening—something very ordinary, but we were listening for what was going on—and that seemed to be something extraordinary. This story had a lot to do with our own stories.

"There was a caravan coming. We thought it was some of those wise guys from the eastside. But the leaders looked smart and serious. They kept looking up at the sky—it was telling some kind of story only they knew. One star stood out above others. Later we found out this was how they were guided in their story."

It was evident many stories were going on in this moment, in this place.

"There were three who came forward in fancy royal duds. They came to the crib where Joshua was lying, and Mary smiling faintly, while Joseph was keeping an eye on the whole thing. Presents were presented (they also told stories): There was gold—something to do with this baby becoming a king; there was incense—something to do with priestly prayers ascending to God; and there was myrrh, a burial spice. They were gifts that would take on meaning as the story unfolded.

"What they didn't know and what they were to find out later was that there was a gift there for them there, lying in a manger—God's gift wrapped in human flesh. This would be understood as they listened to the Story that would give meaning to all their stories."

Well, there we all were, gathered around the old stone fireplace at Uncle Don's and Aunt Pat's. By now most of the grown-ups were getting a bit tipsy and silly or arguing over politics and such. As per tradition my grandpa Willie and grandma Lizzie got up to dance. She put her finger on his bald head and spun him around (which was not a good thing to do when you've had a snoot full). And as per tradition, sooner or later, no matter where the Christmas tree had been placed, Willie found a way to fall into it—thus creating more stories to be told in years to come.

But in the midst of the chaos that ensued, some were still listening as others were telling their own stories:

- Cousin Matt, from the IRS, was over in the corner telling the Story with a Jewish twist to our Jewish Uncle Herman, who was listening with a playful gleam in his eye.
- Cousin Luke, the doctor, was telling the Story to some foreign visitors, English-as-second-language folks—telling how the Story was happening in their cultures. (He'd written two volumes on it.)
- Cousin Johnny, the philosopher, was explaining the Greek *logos* principle to some intellectuals from the Mediterranean area—how God's Word became flesh and really did live among us—and was worth more than a thousand words.

As for me, I was still there, sitting on the rug in front of the fireplace with a few of my cousins. I was listening to Aunt Jenny's old manger up on the mantel tell the Story.

As *I listened I learned:*

- Everyone has an interesting story.
- I need to slow down and listen carefully to other people's stories—to keep my antenna up for what God is doing or wanting to do—to look for His fingerprints.
- I need to listen to my own story—to recognize God's fingerprints throughout my life and let them shape the rest of my story.
- Most of all I need to listen to God's Story and how it intersects with all of our stories—it's what makes sense of our lives, gives meaning to our days, and gives us ways to live on purpose.
- The Jesus story makes sense of all things for me: *"God really was in Christ reconciling the world to Himself."*

As the world clamors for more toys and louder festivities, this is the time to seek the silence, the sacred—even for a few moments. *For it would seem the Author has written Himself into His Story to save us, so that we might live happily ever after.*

Playing the Hand You're Dealt
~12~

"Fear not! For I am with you.
Do not be discouraged, for I am your God.
I will strengthen you, and help you.
I will hold you up with my victorious right hand."[42]

Six years ago: My dad had a stroke and descended into dementia. Every Sunday eve we used to talk on the phone for over an hour—shared memories, stories, and laughter. All are now lost. Sometimes the happy pills worked; other times he was just an angry old man and alone. Recently he moved on. I miss my dad.

Five years ago: My wife, Kathy, was diagnosed with an aggressive breast cancer. There had been two years of remission, but the cancer has returned in the lymph glands in her sternum, lungs, and aorta. The future is a different color these days.

Four years ago: I was diagnosed with vocal cord paralysis. After nine operations, I still never know if a voice will come out in the morning. To you who've graciously put up with hoarse, croaking sermons, and hundreds of gulps of water—I am grateful. I miss having a voice.

Three years ago: I was diagnosed with Parkinson's disease. Among other challenges is standing in the pulpit: My left leg will go numb and my left foot will clench, so I have to balance while speaking—it's kind of like the Godfather meets the Karate Kid.

My doctor prescribed some meds. I asked if there were any side effects. He said that a few people experienced an overwhelming urge for sex and gambling. I said: "I already have that problem, Doc!" To which he replied: "What happens in Vegas stays in Vegas."

Two years ago, my best friend of thirty-five years fell down a dark hole from which he could not get out. He died recently—of a broken heart. I miss my friend.

This year, I lost my job. Poor economic conditions and political power struggles resulted in my position being cut. I'm not sure what's next. As my wife says: "We've both turned sixty, I have cancer, and you have Parkinson's. You're a minister without a voice. Who would want us?" My only reply: "God?"

So this is the hand my wife and I have been dealt. But mysteriously, we are okay—all is well with our souls—we've seen God's fingerprints.

Over the past five years, I've had the privilege of being asked to play in a poker game with some interesting gentlemen from our former church.

Harry, in the middle of dealing the cards, often launched into war stories. Barney would eventually have to interrupt him: "Deal, Harry!"

Barney would often insert a theology question into the game: "George, why are you teaching the book Revelation?" To which I would always reply, "Because it's the most encouraging book in the Bible to me." Barney would scoff, and next game the same banter would arise.

And Al was there. He would mostly just chuckle about all of it.

They each had a "tell"—a mannerism that would tell whether they had good cards or were bluffing. Al was the easiest to tell. When he had good cards, his eyebrows would rise, along with his hat. When Harry had good cards, his face beamed. When he was bluffing, it was written all over his face—he is "a man in whom there is no guile." Barney was shrewder. He would tell folks how good a poker player I was—I think he was trying to make me overconfident so as to overplay my hand (but he'd never tell).

And they all told stories.

I learned a lot about life from playing poker with such characters (the game was fun, but mostly I came for the stories). More than poker, their stories showed how to play the hands we're dealt in life.

You'd think that strong cards would win every time, but you can win with weak cards if you know how to deal with the hand you're dealt. So it is with the challenges of life: we are dealt strong cards and weak cards—what's important is how we play the hand we're dealt.

I'd like to share some of the ways I am learning to play our challenging hand in life. I'll deal you seven cards and hope that at least one of them might help you play the hand you've been dealt.

1st Card: Get a Sense of Humor (The Joker)

"Your wife has stage four cancer—how can you crack jokes?" some might say.

Laughter can keep things in perspective. Life is too important to be taken seriously. I was in Target, right after the cancer diagnosis, and saw two women arguing over a Kleenex box. I thought, *Now here are some people who need a* real *problem. They could learn something from some folks we have met along the cancer journey...*

Glow-in-the-Dark Express

They gather in Harbor City at 3:00 every day—all shapes and sizes, colors and ages—all with one thing in common: they have some kind of cancer that needs radiation. Fifteen people board a shuttle that heads through LA traffic to the hospital in Hollywood. It's about a forty-five-minute trip. I call it the Glow-in-the-Dark Express.

Along the way they tell stories: An 82-year-old Italian woman with a brain tumor jumped out of a plane for her eightieth birthday (she brought pictures); the African-American mailman, shy at first, told of growing up as the only black in his school. He played on the basketball team, but it was difficult because all the white kids "looked alike." He wound up encouraging the Caucasian woman on the bus who was worried about the wounds her cat had inflicted on her dog.

Over the five-week, every weekday trip, folks begin to share: One brings chocolate for everybody, another makes a hat, another shares a book.

When the driver drives a little crazy, or the brakes go out, or they have a near accident, they laugh and scheme practical jokes, and some even pray.

When they arrive, each person goes through their period of radiation. They wait for each other. Though it might take a while, they wait until the last person is done before they head for home.

And they celebrate their hope. On the last day of my wife's radiation, as she stepped on the shuttle, they all applauded.

This handful of human beings has been walking through the valley of the shadow of death together, and as they do, they glow in the dark—in more ways than one. Fingerprints all over the place!

Laughter can be healing: "*A merry heart does good, like a medicine. But a broken spirit dries the bones.*" Proverbs 17:22

My last memory of Mae (who was suffering from encephalitis and lung cancer) was in the ladies' restroom. Mae was sitting on a chair near the mirror, calling out to me and cracking jokes. We were laughing when I said, "Mae, we're in the ladies' restroom," which sent her into hysterics. There we were, partying like five-year-olds when hope arrives (and for Mae and me, it had). Laughter can be healing.

Laughter can also be a weapon of the spirit, defying fear and death. We can laugh because we know that in the end we are holding the winning card. We're betting on the resurrection.

2ⁿᵈ Card: Cultivate Gratitude

The Apostle Paul (who was dealt some very difficult hands) said, "*Give thanks <u>in</u> all things for this is the will of God for you in Christ Jesus.*"[43]

Kathy and I have had five years of unexpected grace (family weekends, holidays, trips to Japan, and our twentieth anniversary in Israel)—it's all been grace. And, therefore, whatever hand we may have been dealt, we are learning how important it is to make the most of each day, each moment, each person, and each opportunity to serve—and to do it thankfully.

3ʳᵈ Card: Choose Your Focus

In Matthew's story (ch. 14): The wind and waves arise, a storm kicks up on the Sea of Galilee, where the disciples, who had been fishing, are now greatly concerned. And here comes Jesus, in the middle of the storm, walking *on* the water. Peter boldly asks, "Lord, bid me to come"—and Jesus does. Lo and behold, Peter is able to walk on the water. When he's focused on Jesus, he is held up. When Peter focuses on the wind and waves, he begins to sink.

Our story the past four years has been: God finds some way, every day, to hold us up. We are being held up by our "scouts"—those who've gone before us and played their difficult hands well; we are held up by "training wheels"—those who come alongside us and steady us when we wobble. We have been held up by all the cards and calls and expressions of care from so many. God shows up, just like we do, in His Body—the Body of Christ—walking on the water— in the storms of life.

It may be a scripture, a book, an encouraging word, a providential circumstance, or an internal whisper of God's spirit, but in some way, every day, we've been held up.

A couple of days ago, I asked my wife how she was. "I'm okay as long as I remember Jesus is in the boat with us. If I look at the storm, I sink."

It's a matter of chosen focus. Will I focus on the storms or the Lord of nature? It's a choice—which comes with a promise: *"Thou wilt keep him in perfect peace whose mind is <u>stayed</u> on thee—why? Because he trusts in Thee."*[44]

4th Card: Keep Moving, Keep Playing, Don't Fold, Don't Quit

Don't get stuck in the valley or lost in the shadow of death. Death is the elephant in everyone's room—casting its shadow on everything. We are intimidated into playing life safe, folding too soon, making weak bets.

Recently I had my first MRI—and it freaked me out. I was stuck in this strange capsule, panicking for fifteen minutes. I finally got out and told the technician I barely made it. She said, "You have twenty more minutes to go." I was ready to run. But she wisely gave me a lifeline to squeeze if I needed to get out, and she patted my foot with assurance that part of my body was already out—which all helped, especially my prayer life.

"Yea, though I walk through the valley of the shadow of death I will fear no evil." Why? *"For Thou art with me."* The Lord really is our shepherd. We can follow Him *through* the valley and out of the shadows, beside still waters, where He restores our souls. Keep moving—stay in the game. This is how we play our hand.

5ᵗʰ Card: Turn Out

When we are dealt difficult cards, the temptation is to turn in on ourselves, like a toothache that commands all our attention. Jesus said, *"If you try to keep your life, you will lose it. If you lose it for my sake, you will find it."* So, turn out! Kathy, after hearing of her bad scan report recently, spent the same afternoon encouraging a mother whose son has brain cancer. My wife continues her bilingual blog: (http://breastcancer.agrainofwheat.org/). A Japanese woman with cancer recently read all three hundred of Kathy's archived entries and wept—and she came to Kathy's cancer support group. Kathy recently visited Japan and met with some cancer patients—folks who were previously strangers, but who had connected through her blog. One woman came to faith in Jesus Christ through reading about Kathy's journey. How do we play a difficult hand? By turning out—serving, comforting, encouraging others.

6ᵗʰ Card: Trust the Process

"We can rejoice, too, when we run into problems and trials, for we know that they help us develop endurance. And endurance develops strength of character, and character strengthens our confident hope of salvation. And this hope will not lead to disappointment."[45]

Rejoice in your sufferings—for they can be productive as we trust that we are in God's hands. What better place to be?

I was able to take woodcarving lessons from a master woodcarver from Oberammergau, Germany. He handed me a block of wood and said, "Make a shoe." I carefully and gently made some small cuts, but with little progress. He took the wood in his hands and made four or five deep cuts—and behold, a shoe!

So it seems to be with suffering. The deep cuts can produce endurance and then character. And a lasting hope is the result of the process. Trusting this process helps in playing the hands we're dealt.

7th Card: Remember God's Faithfulness

Remembering God's faithfulness in our past helps us play our hand in the present and future.

This is a biblical pattern: God did X in the past (cf. Exodus or Jesus); therefore, trust God to be so and do so in the present.

Examples of recent faithfulness: Through Kathy's blog and our continued prayers, we were led to Dr. M—a liver specialist in Japan who has the same kind of cancer as Kathy. Dr. M is the one who came up with the chemo combination that worked, causing a two-year remission.

This year we wanted to go to Israel for our twentieth anniversary, but were not making much progress in our plans. Then we had lunch with my brother and his wife, who heard our story. They said they were going to Israel the next month, had room, and invited us to come. The path cleared for us to go. My mom gave us an unexpected gift, which paid for the trip. And we got to renew our vows in Cana of Galilee, where Jesus did His first miracle—at a wedding.

It's important to remember these things. God is faithful and will be faithful—you can bet on it! Jeremiah said to the discouraged exiles of Israel: *"I know the plans I have for you, says the Lord. They are plans for good and not disaster, to give you a future and a hope."*[46]

Conclusion:
Cancer does not have the last word—God does.
We need not be ruled by the elephant in the room.
Death has been defeated. Death has lost its sting.
Our ace-in-the-hole is the resurrection of Jesus.

We are at peace knowing we are in God's hands—what better place to be! We are being held up by God and His people, and we trust that God has our best in mind, that He is wiser than we are, so therefore we say, "Thy will be done!"

Kathy continues to honor God and serve others. She will not be taken until God's purpose is fulfilled (that's why we're all here anyway). Then, onto a new body and being with the Lord forever—"In his presence there is fullness of joy." Not a bad deal! Death has been swallowed up in victory, of that we are confidently hopeful.

Meanwhile, we will play the hand we've been dealt: making the most of each moment, each person, each opportunity we are given—and living gratefully, remembering God's faithfulness, giving thanks in all things. We'll keep moving and turning out, trusting the process and keeping our eyes on Jesus. So, as you play the hand *you've* been dealt:

"Fear not! For I am with you.
Do not be discouraged, for I am your God.
I will strengthen you, and help you.
I will hold you up with my victorious right hand."

It's your deal—ante up!

Dusting for God's Fingerprints
Postlude

What I have learned from Mr. Toad's wild ride (thus far)...

God is a jazz musician weaving the messes of our existence into meaningful tunes, creating order out of our chaos, jamming His heart out to redeem us.

I just need to remember: "It don't mean a thing if it ain't got that swing!"

The Bible is a simple story: God made us, we got lost, God has come to find us and bring us home. The End! (And the Beginning.)

Humanity is like the WWF: Job in this corner, hell beaten out of him, God in the other corner. He has come blowing into the ring of our age-old arguments, saying, "Gird up your loins and wrestle like a man!" There, in our corner, a lion roaring—coming down into our struggle. Awesome dignity and humility have arrived—the Father you always wanted. Job and I and you asking the big questions that in the end do not matter—they are eclipsed by a passionate Presence, which in the end is all that does matter.

Salvation is like the little Japanese boy who just had his chest cracked open and a new heart stuffed into the center of his being (something we all need in one way or another.). He and I (who can't understand a word of each other's language) there in front of a fireplace, popping popcorn, and sharing the wonder of it together—there in front of us a mini big-bang of new creation going on—with butter and salt running down our elbows—both of just glad to be alive—just like in the beginning.

Jesus, our Savior, is like Superman becoming Clark Kent in order to save a bunch of Clark Kents who think they are supermen. Yet who by grace might just become Jimmy Olsen, filled with wonder at it all. And somewhere on this Daily Planet, there is a church being sought for a bride—will Lois Lane ever get it? As Perry White would say, Great Caesar's ghost!

The church is like a blues club in Watts where my son and I have hung out from time to time. There's an old gentleman, 80 years young, decked to the nines and announcing, "I am the host!" (repeating it with every guest's entrance.) It's good to be welcomed. There's a 90-year-old lady named Babe who owns and opens the club just for the life of it. And there's the cat's a jammin', offering up their licks for all to hear. And of course there's Miss Mickey beltin out them blues—3 parts Hennesey.s, 1 part acetylene torch. God'sa cryin' out for His people, she's struttin' her stuff between what's left of a few broken teeth—and telling the stories, declaring "I am your living legend". Sometimes she gets confused with the Christ, but it's ok, he don't mind—he's enjoying the music, the folks, the fried chicken, and the jokes—like the young white boy next to me who says he doesn't know why they call it the blues when it makes him happy—And with that the musicians can pack up and go home—they've done their job—been true to their gifts and callings—God's been here and done that—fingerprints.

Word: There is a Story in the midst—stories within the Story, or Story within stories, or both. They invite, even seem to write my story. I see myself in the Word, the world through it, God in and beyond it—though most times darkly. I find hope and meaning and questions—and I question the hope and meaning—and find hope and meaning in the questioning. I find a framework living and working, relating and thinking, and sinning and saving, and praying and doubting in this here Word of God. In the scriptures I see psalms and blues and screams and dreams and different hues of jazz refrains—I feel the poetic pushing me out beyond the safe places and into the land of the living.

There's some pointing and hinting and truth-ringing and inklinging—sometimes even yelling going on. "Wake up!" the prophets shout, addressing me and the world and sometimes even God. Sometimes I just see truth standing there, naked in all His glory. These texts and textures are startlingly honest and honestly startling—busting out the seams on my calculated life of illusive securities. And here I am trying to figure out how much freedom I can stand when a gust of Spirit-wind carries me out there into the great unknown and sometimes the greater known—it is sometimes a scary place.

But we are not left alone. Spirit comes alongside us, the Comedian and Cosmic Joker who sometimes smacks me right between the eyes, sometimes in this old hard heart. Most times He just nudges me from behind and whispers, "Tag, you're it"—leaving only fingerprints.

All these prints just point to God, our Father. There seems to be some purposively passionate poet, carefully careless craftsman, foolishly frustrated lover, a waiting Father behind and within and before and beyond it all.

This creative wind comes blowing through words and silences, through my mind and sometimes into my very heart and soul—sometimes even right into my flesh and bones. Sometimes Father-Son-Spirit kicks up a storm between you and me, and lightning splinters common events, revealing splendor in the ordinary. Thunder causes me, awes me, to stop and wonder out loud.

Eschatologically (Toad word) speaking, I sense a father-son or husband-wife argument going on in the universe. And there's a resolution somewhere in there and in here, somewhat now, and a lot more later. I hope, therefore I am.

I smell a giant cosmic poker game in which God is dealing and playing and we've been invited to play. And though sometimes we feel like losers, there's a card up His sleeve called resurrection, which seems to be the ace in the hole of just about everybody's heart. I think it's time to ante up.

Eternal life is a flesh-wrapped gift containing prizes and puzzles, mysterious directions, unexpected lessons, party invitations and favors. For some: blank-stare nonresponses; for others: spine-tingling *Aha* moments. Must be some kinda party, wouldn't ya say!

Heaven: It's finally laughter, for joy is the serious business of heaven—by those who knew it not. And it's no more tears for those who know them all too well, who've been to the well, and to the wall. It's promises made and promises to keep—and it points to the miles until we sleep in the everlasting arms of the kind and the clever—until we wake in the eternal joy of having been loved forever.

Well, that's some of what I learned from all those fingerprints.

Sometimes Mr. Toad's wild ride gets weary. Sometimes we're tempted to give up, to give in. There's enough good reason. And yet… Maybe there's still some good news in that old Gospel for me and you. Maybe grace will find a way to save all of us toads—the whole kit and kaboodle! Maybe we'll all love happily ever after, after all.

We are a people of hope. We believe the promise of one who will come, like the young lady did in eighth grade, and dance with us old toads—but as you know from the fairy tales, only frogs become princes. We toads when kissed by grace turn into servants. Our hero is the one who stoops, who takes up the towel and basin and washes feet—who came not to be served, but to serve and give his life for many. My aim is to be among you as one who serves.

Conclusion;

Well, that's a little bit of my story. I hope it might help you to listen to your own life and discover some of God's fingerprints. For in the end all of our stories will be woven into a much bigger story—God's Story.

Credits and Sources

1. Kenneth Grahame, *The Wind in the Willows*, Charles Scribner's Sons. 1908, 1933, 1953.

2. Matthew 6:33.

3. George W. Baum.

4. Luke 22:32.

5. Genesis 12-20.

6. *The Wind in the Willows*.

7. Genesis 12:1.
    Ch. 1 Concept Source: Mark Twain, *Extracts from Adam's Diary*, Harper & Brothers, 1906.

8. Genesis 3:4.

9. Genesis 12.

10. G.K. Chesterton, *Orthodoxy*, Image Books, 1959, pp. 120-121.

11. Psalm 126:5.

12. Luke 6:21.

13. Frederick Buechner, *Whistling in the Dark*, Harper & Row, 1988, p. 29.

14. John Shea, *An Experience Named Spirit*, Intro.

15. C.S. Lewis.

16. Quoted by C.H. Spurgeon.

17. Jeremiah 18:1-6.

18. Jeremiah 18:6.

19. Romans 8:28.

20. Squire Rushnell, *When God Winks,* Atria/Simon & Schuster, 2002.

21. The Marsalis story might be apocryphal.

22. Lamentations 1-3.

23. Lamentations 1.

24. Lamentations 3.

25. Lamentations 3:21-24.

26. Frederick Buechner, *Wishful Thinking*, Harper & Row, 1973, pp 33-34.

27. "Story of Grace," Delmar Leger, ServantsNews.com, 2002.

28. Lamentations 3:54-57.

29. Romans 8:28.

30. John 12:24.

31. Matsuo Basho.

32. Ezekiel 37.

33. "Power for Resolution," Gordon Cosby, *Handbook for Mission Groups*, 1975, p. 90.

34. Proverbs 12:18.

35. Frederick Buechner, *Secrets in the Dark.* HarperCollins, 2006.

36. Ephesians 4:32.

37. Revelation 21:5.

38. Revelation 19:9.

39. Revelation 21:1.

40. "The Magnificat," Luke 1.

41. Psalm 23.

42. Isaiah 41:6-10.

43. I Thessalonians 5:18.

44. Isaiah 26:3.

45. Romans 5: 3-4.

46. Jeremiah 29:11.

CPSIA information can be obtained
at www.ICGtesting.com
Printed in the USA
FSOW01n0634121115
13305FS